WROUGHTON HISTORY

PART 1

Studies in the history of Wroughton Parish

by

Wroughton History Group

Front cover: Yew tree cottage, Priors Hill, by Sandra Curtis.

Published by Wroughton History Group

   The Library
   Wroughton
   Wilts

ISBN 0 9508393 0 2

© Copyright Wroughton History Group 1982
Copyright of individual studies specific to each author
Parish schools may use extracts for educational purposes

Printed by Timeprint Ltd.,
         172 Rodbourne Road
         Swindon
         SN2 2AF

Foreword

It is with considerable interest that I have read Wroughton History.
Those responsible for its compilation are to be congratulated on
the considerable amount of time they have spent on research and the
putting together of the results of their work and study.

Wroughton is a place that has changed considerably since I came to
live at Overtown in 1948 and those pre-war residents will, of
course, have noticed even more dramatic changes. With the
diversification of industry in Swindon and its rapid expansion,
Wroughton was bound to lose its more rural outlook and become a
dormitory area for Swindon. With the advent of the R.A.F. in 1938,
and the increase in road traffic, it became impossible to train
racehorses which for a long period had provided an interest and
employment for residents. Possibly a threat to their incomes,
trying to find local winners, has been removed!

I believe this History will provide nostalgic memories for the
older residents and great interest for those new residents who
study History. We should be grateful indeed to those who have
produced it.

Sir Henry Calley. D.S.O. and D.F.C.

September 1982

Acknowledgements

Without the help of the following the book could never have been completed and we are most grateful to all of them, as well as to the many individuals who lent photographs or books, or gave information or advice.

W.E.A. organiser Bob Emmett
Peter Good
Paul Henderson
John Gaunt
May Shinn
Mrs Cripps
Mr T Dalglish
Wendy Jones
Ridgeway School
Dr B Lawton of Highworth Historical Society
Wroughton Library Staff
The Library and Museum Service
and especially to J.H. Bettey who gave alot of his time and expertise to keep us on the right track throughout the compiling of this book.

Joyce Hamilton
W.W. Rouch & Co.
Wiltshire Newspapers

We are grateful for the sponsorship of
HAMBRO LIFE CHARITABLE TRUST
BARRETTS OF WROUGHTON
G CLEVERLEY and Partners
MR PROSSER
MR & MRS A ENTWISTLE
P. ELLIOTT
Mr & MRS C. WILSON

We are indebted to local shops for agreeing to sell this book for us without commission:

WROUGHTON P.O.
NORTH WROUGHTON P.O.
BORLAYS NEWSAGENTS
GORDONS
RUSSELLS of Fleet Street.
FOSTERS of Wootton Bassett.

PUBLISHED WITH THE SUPPORT OF WROUGHTON PARISH COUNCIL

List of Subscribers

MR K.S. ABSALOM
G.W. ALLEN
F.E. ALVIS
J. ARCHER
MRS K. AUDRITT

MR D.J. ADAMS
R.D. ALLEN
MRS P. ANDRESS
B.G.E. ARGENT
S.F. AUSTIN

W.R. ADAMS
MR & MRS S.J. ALLEN
MISS J. ARCHER
J. ARNOLD

MRS J. BAILEY
J. BALDWIN
MR & MRS R.W. BARRETT
MR & MRS G.H. BAZELY
J. BEVIR
MR & MRS S. BOON
C.G. BRAIN
L.T. BROUGH
MR J. BURFORD
MRS H.I. BUTLER

MRS BAKER
S. BARLOW
E.S. BARTLEY
IAN G. BELL
S.W. BOLDEN
MRS C. BOWN
MR & MRS J. BRAWLEY
MR DAVID BROWN
MR & MRS R.J. BURLISON
MR J.E. BUTLER

DAPHNE BAKER
MR & MRS JEFF BARRETT
K. BATES
D.S. BERRY
MRS J. BONHAM
ANN BRADLEY
J. BROOKS
MRS E.A. BROWN
G.F. BUTLER

R.H. CAIRNS
MR C. CARD
MR C. CHIVERS
C.J. CLINCH
MRS J.A. COLE
MRS B. COMMANDER
MRS G. COOMBS
S. CRISP
MRS MAXINE CULLINGWORTH
MR & MRS W. CURTIS

SIR HENRY CALLEY
MRS B.J. CARTER J.P
L.J. CLARK
MISS CODRINGTON
MRS. COLLINS
CHRISTOPHER C. COOK
MISS B.M. COPPIN
MR & MRS ADRIAN C. CROCKER
A.H. CURTIS

MRS J. CALNAN
CAVERN VENTURE SCOUTS
MR & MRS CLARK
MRS P. COHEN
MRS P. COLMAN, LIBRARIAN
MR. S.S. COOK
MRS A.P. CRISP
MISS MARION CROWDY
M.A. CURTIS

W. DA CUNHA
J.G. DAVIS
D.H. DAY
MRS S. DE ROSA
MR & MRS S. DICKENS
MRS M. DRAYSON
MRS G.F. DUNN

H.G. DANIELS
P.DAVIS
MRS DELLER
MRS J.P. DEVITT
W.E. DONNELLY
MR & MRS D. DRISCOLL
H.S. DUNSCOMBE

MICHAEL J. DANIELS
R.A. DAVIS
MR & MRS P.V. DERBYSHIRE
MRS IRIS DICKENS
DAVID R. DOUBLEDAY
MRS A. DUCKWORTH

CAROLINE EAGLING
PETER ILLIOTT
JEAN EVANS

MRS I. EDMONDS
MRS M. ELLIS
M. EVANS

MRS B.J. ELLIOTT
E. ENTWISTLE

C. FERRIMAN
MRS F.A. FISHER
J.F. FISHLOCK
D.J. FLINTHAM
A.J. FOSTER

MR N.C.B. FIELDER
MRS P. FISHER
MRS D.W. FITCHETT
MARK FLOYD
MR K. FREEGARD

MRS F. FILES
VERA L. FISHER
DR. C.A. FLEMING
T. FORD
MR W.S. FRENCH

P.N. GAMBLE
MR & MRS J.S. GIBBS
MR F.J. GODDARD
N.J. GOSLING
J.W. GREENAWAY
MR N. GREY

MR R.J. GARRAWAY
MRS M. GINGELL
MRS S. GODFREE
MRS J. GOUGH
MRS D. GREENSHIELDS
GARY GRUBB

H.E. GARRETT
MRS E. GODDARD
F.J. GOSLING
NORMAN GOUGH
A.S. GREENWOOD

MRS I. HABGOOD
MRS JOYCE HAMILTON
MRS M.S. HASKINS
M. HAYNES
MRS E.M. HENNESSY
MRS P. HICKS
H.F. HORTON
MRS V. HUTCHINS

MRS E. HACKER
G.F. HARRIS
T.W.F. HATCHER
V.R. HAYNES
MR C.W. HEXT
MRS J.A. HOBBS
MR T. HOWELLS

MRS M. HALL
MRS M. HARRY
M.E. HAYES
PEGGY HAYWARD
D. HICKS
W.C.R. & P.D. HORSELL
MRS R. HUMPHRIES

MR R. ILES
H. JARMAN
R.A. JEPHSON
MRS B. JOHNSON
MRS JOSIE JONES

MR D. JAMES
MR F.R. JEFFERIES
MR JERROM
VALERIE JOHNSTONE

MR T. JAMES
I.K. JEFFERIES
MRS JOHNS & MRS GREGORY
ERNEST F. JONES

P. KEAY
MRS M. KELLY
JOSEPHINE & HARRY KEMBLE
BETTY KENT
MR R. KENT
MRS W.M. KERR
MR & MRS G.C. KIDD
MR & MRS S.J. KINGHORN
DOROTHY KNOPP

O.M. LAW
PAT LEACH
G.R. LEIGHFIELD
MISS M. LEIGHFIELD
JEAN LEO
ROSEMARY LEO
MRS LE PAGE
MR D.C. LEWIS
MRS P. LEWIS
S.P. LEWIS
JUNE R. LILLEY
MR F.A. LINFIELD
MR & MRS LINNEY
MRS J. LITTLE
MR & MRS LONG
MISS M. LOUDWILL
REV. R. LUCAS
MR & MRS C. LUCY
MR P.J. LUNDY

MRS M.A. McCORMICK
MR & MRS W. MCKANAN-JONES
R.A. & P.M. McMEEKING
SARAH McMEEKING
BARRY R. MARCHANT
MRS B. MASON
MRS S.A. MENDHAM
M.J. MIDDLETON
MRS MILES
MRS F. MILLARD
MRS F.R. MOON
MARJORIE & RICHARD MOORE
MRS R.J. MORSE
MRS W. MORSE
MRS I. MORTON
L.B. MOSS
H. MURRAY
MR R.R. MYERS

MRS C. NEGUS
F.C. NELMES
J. NEWBURY
G.H. NEWMAN
MRS E.M. NOKE
MR M.P. NOLAN
MR R. NORTON
H.J.B. NUTT

MR K.W. ODY
MR M.C. O'LEARY

STEPHANIE PAIGE
MRS J. PAINTER
MRS JEAN PAINTER
R.W. PAINTER
E.K. PALMER
J.A. PALMER
A.E. PARKER
MR K. PARSONS
MRS A.M. PEARCE
MRS M. PENFOUND
MR & MRS R. PENTNEY
P.G. PENZER
DAVID PHIPPS
MR N.S. PILKINGTON
MRS K.W. PILL
D.R. PILLINGER
MR J.J. PILLINGER
MGR GEORGE PITT
R. PLEVEY
TREVOR PONTING
MRS G. POOLE
MR L. POTTER
MR DAVID POUNDER
MRS J. POUNDER
MRS H. POWELL
MRS M. POWER
MRS K.M. PRATT
MR & MRS D.J. PREDDY
MRS E. PREECE
PETER WILLIAM PROSSER
W.H. PROSSER
MR & MRS R. PROUDLEY
MRS C.A. PURDON

MRS M.E. RAYNER
S. REES
MRS SHEILA REES
MRS S. RIBBINS
ANN RICHARDS
MRS I. RICHINGS
A ROBBINS
C.L. ROBINSON
MRS M.J. ROGERS
MRS ROWE
MR & MRS J. ROWE
MR RUMBLE
JOHN RUMMING
PETER RUMMING

MRS B.H. SALTER
S.H. SALTER
P.A. SANSUM
MRS JOAN SAUNDERS
MR P.K. SCOTT
MR W. SEAR
G.P. SHAW
M. SHINN
MR S.H. SHOWELL
MRS C.J. SIMPSON-GEE
P.A.F. SIMS
JOAN SMART
MR F.W.J. SMITH
J.H. SMITH
LILIAN F.J. SMITH
MAJOR & MRS M.C. SMITH
MR R.J. SMITH
R.R. SMITH
MRS MURIEL SOUTHERN
D. STAFFORD
MRS DOREEN STARK
H. STARR
MR I.J. STEPHENS
MR R. STEVENS
F.W. STOCKING
K.M. STODDART
MR M.J. STONE
L. STORRAR
MRS M. STRANGE
E.J. STROUD
N.S.M. STURLA
J.N. SUTTON
MR & MRS G.B. SWATTON
MISS J.L.H. SWATTON

MRS D. TEBBUTT
N.P. THACKERAY
MRS E. THOMAS
W. THOMAS
W.R. TIDBALL
MR A.W. TOVEY
CHRISTINE TURNBULL
DR GORDON TURNBULL
MR & MRS K.J. TURNBULL
MRS D.A. TYLER

D & J VINCENT
A.B. WALLACE
MRS E.M. WALTERS
ERICA WALTON
MRS J.C. WARD
H.E. WATTS
MRS HAZEL WEBB
MRS M.E. WEBB
G.J. WEBBER
KEITH WESTON
MR A. WHARTON
MR & MRS F. WHATLEY
MRS B. WHEELER
N.C. & L.A. WHELAN
DR J.H. WHITE
MRS M. WHITEHEAD
J. WHITING
MRS M. WICK
MRS P.M. WILLIAMS
MR A. WILLIAMSON
E. WILLIAMSON
MR & MRS C. WILSON
WINTERBOURNE CONSTRUCTION
LIMITED
A.J. WIRDNAM

MISS B. WITCOMBE
ROSE WITTS
MISS B.M. WOOD
MR M. WOODWARD
MRS P. WOODWARD
MRS N.G. WRIGHT
MRS WRIXON

MRS D. YOUNG
MR K.W.D. YULE

CONTENTS

MAPS

1. Wroughton Church Hill looking North East (Wilts. Newspapers)

INTRODUCTION

by

Diane Gibbs

In 1977 the Swindon branch of the Workers' Educational Association organised a course on "The History of Wroughton" at our new library. The course was well attended. Most people, however, had expected to be supplied with a ready-made history, and it soon became apparent that, apart from reminiscences of older members of the class, there would be nothing specific to Wroughton; but for those who were really interested in the subject, this would be only a guide for their own researches.

This course was followed by another on "Landscape History", from which a small group set out to apply their efforts to the Parish of Wroughton. The progress was erratic and the objective not too clear. However after a large amount of material had been collected, it was felt that it had become essential to put some of it into published form, so that it would not be lost. This book is, therefore, only a beginning, and it is hoped to publish more periodically.

. . . .

Wroughton parish is part of a county which has been called the 'cradle of early civilization of this country'. One has only to look at such tourist attractions as Avebury, Stonehenge and West Kennet Long Barrow, to note the antiquity of the area.

The Parish of Wroughton is situated in the north-east of the County of Wiltshire. Four of its five manors were in the Ancient Hundred of Blackgrove, whose meeting place, according to the Place Names of Wiltshire, 'must have been at Blackgrove Farm' in Wroughton. This Hundred has now been absorbed by the Kingsbridge Hundred. The fifth manor, Wroughton Manor, which was held by the Prior of St. Swithin's, Winchester, was contained in the Hundred of Elstub.

In the Anglo-Saxon Chronicle of 890 A.D. ELLENDUN was the name of a large part of land now known as Wroughton. Ellendun probably meant elder-tree down, (favoured by the Place Names Society), although it could possibly have meant enclosure or fort of Ella, (Wiltshire Notes and Queries). The boundary is described in Codex Dipl. 1184 - 956 A.D. as follows:-

> "First from the heathen burial place and along the
> way to Cress-combe, thence to the cow pasture; from the cow
> pasture to the Ridgeway, from the Ridgeway to Ealhere's
> burying place, thence and along the ditch to Hawkthorn,
> from the thorn to the broad stone, thence to the clover mere,
> from the mere to Helmesthorn. From the thorn to the brook, thence
> to the Elder stumps, from the Stumps to the Church highway, thence
> to Rhudwylle, from Rhudwylle to Hrysanbeorge, from the barrow to
> Cold barrow, from the barrow and along the way to the Stone,
> from the Stone again to the heathen burial place."

This is the only remaining Anglo Saxon Charter we have for the Parish, although names used in the Domesday Book (1086) for other portions might be applicable to the other manors, e.g. Wertune and Wervetone.

It was not until 1496 that the Church was called Wroughton, alias - otherwise called - Elyndon Church. Today's name of WROUGHTON means 'farm on the River WORF'. Worf is an old name for the River Ray, used in 962 A.D. and its root name suggest that it twists and turns. There have been many variations over the years, (which could produce a study in itself), and in 1620 it was known in documents, both as Elington alias Wroughton and Wroughton alias Elingdon.

Why did ancient man travel and settle in this area? The answer lies in the geology of the area, the type of rock which forms the soil, the chalk.

Chalk downs are hilly areas (Barbury Castle is at a height of 871 ft. above sea level) covered by a dry springy turf, a distinct advantage, for the traveller, over damp, boggy clay vales which were once clad with oak trees and dense thorny undergrowth, and the haunt of wolves.

The chalk provided many trade routes, e.g. with Dorset, Kent, East Anglia and Yorkshire, as shown on the sketch map, and all of them met on the Marlborough Downs, which gave the area great importance. Incidentally the Ridgeway was formerly known as the "Walceway" - that is the Welsh or foreigner's way.

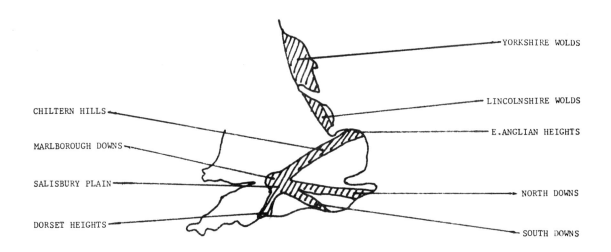

Because of their height, the downs also gave a clear view over a great distance, so that a surprise attack on itinerant traders was most unlikely. It was for this reason, also, that the fortified camps of Liddington, Uffington and Barbury were placed on the ridges of the downs. Note the extensive views from Barbury on a clear day.

Stone Age man found flints amongst the chalk and used them, after shaping, as tools and weapons, a great advance on bare hands.

There is evidence of Celtic fields on the eastern slopes below Barbury Castle and also at Fyfield. These were under cultivation during the Iron Age and continued in use through the Roman Period. If one travels up Burderop Hill to Barbury when the sun is low, it is possible to see these small, square fields. (see plate 27).

The dry trackways also allowed people to travel and meet others (when life was sufficiently organised) at specially constructed henges such as Avebury and Stonehenge. Avebury is the largest henge monument in Britain, and consists of enormous sarsen stones, which have been manhandled from the chalk, where they were found. The outer ring of Stonehenge is also composed of sarsens. The sarsens, themselves, are thought to have once covered the chalk, but the layer has now been mainly eroded.

With all these advantages, therefore, it was no accident that Wiltshire was chosen by early man for his 'home'.

Boundaries

The Parish of Wroughton is of an irregular shape and has been altered several times in recent years. In 1956, the acreage was 6950 (compared with Swindon's 6060) and in 1973 had increased to 7109. The Borough of Thamesdown was created on the 1st April 1974, since when there have been several reductions in acreage to Wroughton Parish.

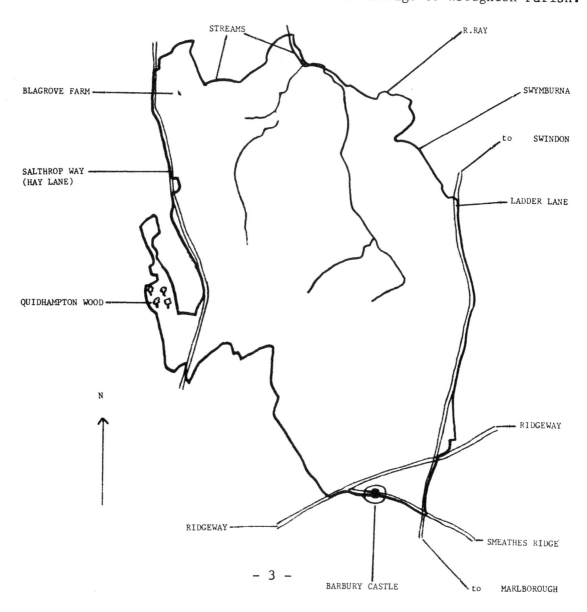

The population numbers of Wroughton and its northern neighbour Swindon, were comparable until the mid Nineteenth Century, when the railway came and New Town developed.

In 1840 most of Wroughton's northern limit was formed by the course of four streams, with a projection northwards away from the stream in the northwest to include Blagrove Farm, the meeting place of Blackgrove Hundred.

The eastern boundary is marked by the old road from Swindon to Barbury Down via Ladder Lane, which was the old paved road to Marlborough before turnpiking took place.

The southern boundary, (formed partly by a trackway called Smeathe's Ridge) is on the chalk of the Marlborough Downs. It has already been suggested that the ancient trackways were sited on dry ridges, as progress would be swifter and safer than in the wooded clay vales.

Smeathe's Ridge passes through the centre of the Iron Age hill fort known as Barbury Castle. It is just one of a string of hill forts in the area, e.g. Liddington, Bincknoll, which indicates the presence of ancient trade routes. Smeathe's Ridge meets the Ridgeway to the west of Barbury Castle, which forms a small part of the boundary and cuts across the south-eastern corner of the parish. For the remainder of this oddly shaped boundary on the downs, no reason is, as yet, apparent.

The western boundary is made partially by yet another ancient road to the downs, Hay Lane, a broad drove road. It follows a straight course from Cricklade to the Ridgeway, a north-south route. This road was known in the Fourteenth Century as the Ancient Way and also as Saltharpesweye. It is still marked by two stones, whose inscriptions have become indecipherable over the years. In this area we have another eccentricity, a long finger-shaped projection (see sketch map) with no firm explanation, as yet.

Geology

The Parish of Wroughton is divided into distinct bands of clay, greensand and chalk, which cut across it from east to west.

The geology of the parish influences the type of agriculture followed, its buildings and its industry. These will all be invest-igated elsewhere in greater detail.

Wroughton Parish is typical of a 'chalk and cheese' parish. The southern half is composed entirely of chalk. The greensand forms a narrow band on a sharp slope. This can be difficult to identify because chalk slips often cover it. On the chalk with its well drained and shallow soil, sheep were kept. They were the long legged Wiltshire Horn, which were bred for mutton and for their ability to walk long distances over the chalk downlands where they fed during the day. At night they walked to the arable lands where they were folded in order to enrich the soil with their dung. More modern methods were intro-duced in 1750. There is little evidence of wool influencing the activities of the area. On the 'cheese', the Kimmeridge and Gault clays, dairying was followed, producing milk and cheese. The cheese was carried to Marlborough market via the old toll road to Barbury and across the downs.

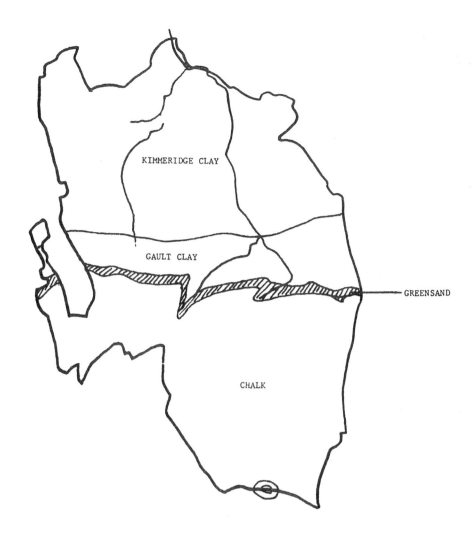

There are several buildings in the parish which make use of chalk blocks, e.g. Laburnum Cottage and Parsloe's Farm, whose footings are of impervious sarsen stones. These are composed of exceedingly hard sandstone and are to be found on the downs amidst the chalk. The sarsens are moved to the field boundaries, where possible, by the farmer.

Chalk quarrying was a skilled job as the blocks had to be prepared carefully before use. Chalk pits can still be seen to the east of the footpath off Prior's Hill. The sarsens themselves once provided a source of employment. In about 1900 they created a thriving industry producing hardcore and pavement edgings. There are some to be seen in the High Street.

The northern half of the parish is clay, of which there are two types: Gault and Kimmeridge.

Of the known brickworks, both have been sited on the Kimmeridge Clay. Why not on the Gault? There are two possible reasons for this: it was in use as farmland and the village was built on it.

Our earliest reference to a brickmaker in Wroughton is that of Mr John Spackman who in 1867 was listed as a beer retailer and brickmaker. Obviously brickmaking was not a regular form of employment at this time. In 1895 we have mention of two brickmakers. Was this a time of extensive brick building in Wroughton? By 1906 there was one brickmerchant and NO brickmakers in the village.

But in 1915 Mr Edward Hill was working as a brick and tile maker.
In a newspaper article written in 1927 by Alfred Williams, it is
stated that "bricks are (or were) cheaper than chalk". This was
possibly because of the time needed to season the chalk blocks and
the effort needed to quarry them, as all the easily available
material had been used.

Settlement

The parish was divided into five tithings. A tithing was an
Anglo-Saxon term for a group of ten free men. Its purpose was to
provide mutual protection and ensure strict observance of the law.

The five tithings were Elcombe, Overtown, Salthrop, Westlecott
(now partly outside the parish) and Wroughton, which would suggest
communities albeit small, in these tithings. See sketch map below for
extent of these tithings.

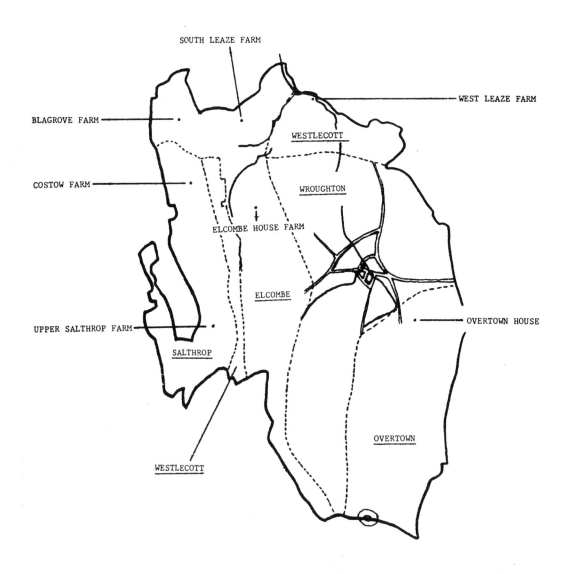

Elcombe forms a long, narrow strip from north to south across all types of soil. South Leaze farmhouse is situated on the clay as was the Blagrove farmstead. Many dwellings were to be found along Elcombe Street, as shown by the population census of 1841, with 348 inhabitants.

Overtown is unusual in the parish, in being sited entirely on chalk. In 1941 it had a population of 78. There are humps and bumps and ditches to the south of Overtown House, showing signs of 'croft and Toft'. This indicates the site of a deserted mediaeval village.

Salthrop tithing forms a strip north to south across the parish to include the Quidhampton Wood eccentricity. Costow farmstead is on the clay, while Upper Salthrop farmhouse and Quidhampton Wood are on the greensand. Salthrop in 1841, had a total of 56 inhabitants. It has been suggested that Quidhampton was a settlement at one time, but was destroyed by a landslip in the Nineteenth Century.

Westlecott, now mainly outside the parish, was a split tithing (see map) with a very narrow band sandwiched between Elcombe and Salthrop tithings, the remaining part being entirely on the clay. There is evidence of another deserted mediaeval village at West Leaze, although there is no present day hamlet.

Wroughton was the largest tithing, containing the church and the main settlement. The original village has developed just below a line of greensand, on the Gault clay. The greensand ensured a good water supply, from the many springs which start there, as the water is unable to percolate through the clay.

The oldest houses today, would appear to be in the region of Green's Lane, Baker's Road and the High Street. Houses have been built, roughly forming a circle, along the A361 (High Street), B4005 (Marlborough Road), Prior's Hill and their connecting lanes.

The modern estates of the 1960s have spread even farther onto the clay, enveloping land and farms; e.g. Coventry Farm and its land, and land belonging to Berkeley Farm. Manor Farm house escaped until the end of the seventies, although its land was taken earlier, and this development is known as Manor Farm Estate.

Individual population figures for each hamlet have not been published, except for the 1841 census, but the total population figures for the parish can be illustrated as follows on the next page, one symbol representing 250 people.

Note the one thousand increase in population between 1951 and 1961, and then the massive building programme resulting in the increase of approximately two thousand, five hundred, between 1961 and 1971.

DATE	NUMBER OF INHABITANTS								
1676	260	�726							
1801	1100								
1811	1202								
1821	1381								
1831	1545								
1841	1963								
1851	1645								
1861	1721								
1871	2087								
1881	2225								
1891	2511								
1901	2448								
1911	2383								
1921	2462								
1931	2641								
1941	No census taken during the war.								
1951	4085								
1961	5108								
1971	7625								
1973	7875								
1976	8050								

(Each figure in the pictograph rows represents a number of inhabitants.)

Dividing lines after groups of 4 = 1000 people

The population figures have now stabilised and as the building of new houses is limited to infilling there is not likely to be any significant increase in the future.

References and Sources of Information

Victoria County History (various volumes).
North Wilts and District Directories.
Ordnance Survey maps.
Geological Survey of G.B., 1857 G.H. Gove, Swindon.
Geology of Wiltshire R.S. Barron.
The Place Names of Wiltshire, J.E.B. Gover, Allen Mawer, F.M. Stanton.
W.I. Scrapbook.
Swindon Museum, Bath Road.
Articles by Mrs Story Maskelyne.
Dr J.H. Bettey.
Article from the Wiltshire Times, October 15, 1927, "Wiltshire
     Village Industries"-No. IV, by Alfred Williams.
Article from "Wiltshire Notes and Queries," Vol. 2
Understanding English Place Names Wm. Addison.

THE CHURCH IN WROUGHTON

by Barbara Pearce

The Parish Church of St. John the Baptist and St. Helen

By far the oldest identifiable site of Christian worship in the Parish is at or closeby the existing Parish Church. It is mentioned in the Anglo-Saxon charter of the Bounds of Ellendune in 956 A.D. that the boundary between the manors of Elcombe and Ellendune from Helen's Thorn (roughly the 700 feet contour on the O.S. Map) to the Church and thence along the line of the still visible double bank running from the Church towards the North.

The Parish comprised, as is recorded elsewhere, five manors, from the principal of which, Elyndon or Ellandune, it took its first name. From the late 15th century it became known as Wroughton alias Elyndon and subsequently Wroughton.

In the Register of John of Pontissara, Bishop of Winchester 1281 - 1304 we are fortunate to find listed the founders of many of the Churches of the area and, in particular "Elyndone quod est Worston" is recorded, founded by King Ethelstan. This would be between 925 - 939 A.D. Athelstan had considerable links with the area and spent much time at Malmesbury. It is most likely that Athelstan's Church replaced an even earlier shrine, for the dedication handed down to us today, to St. John the Baptist and St. Helen, is unusual.

Compound dedications are not particularly uncommon especially in Wessex and the Celtish parts of the country, which were strongholds of the Celtish form of the faith (Note). It has been frequent for the name of a biblical or canonical saint to be added to a dedication when the fame of the original dedicatee has faded and, in particular, Henry VIII encouraged the changing of many dedications. It has been argued that the Helen of the dedication is Helen, mother of the Emperor Constantine and reputed finder of the true Cross. However, though it is known that Helen, who was probably a Briton and certainly a Christian, founded many Churches in Yorkshire and Lincolnshire especially while her husband and later, son, were stationed at York, it has never been shown that either she or Constantine visited Wessex so it seems unlikely that the name refers to her. Considering though the recurrent incidence of the name Ella or Ellen in names in the locality it seems more likely that Ellen or Helen was a local Celtic "saint" commemorated at the early shrine and whose memory was perpetuated in the dedication handed down to us today.

Situated as it is, on the boundaries of the old manors of Elcombe and Ellendune, the Church is at the centre of the Parish. A high point was traditionally chosen by the Celts for the site of a holy place possibly so that it could be seen from as wide an area as possible and identified as the shrine, or perhaps to provide a landmark or beacon, or even to provide a stronghold. In this instance the area is known as Wroughton Castle. The configuration of the land has been said to suggest the vallum and fossa of an ancient hill fort in parts, but there is no archaeological evidence to support this. Only mediaeval pottery has been found in the banked area.

Note: One of the most complicated is that of Winchester Abbey, originally dedicated to St. Amphibalus, SS Peter and Paul and St. Swithin. St. Amphibalus was then dropped at the time of the Conquest as in the sixteenth century Henry VIII changed it to The Sacred and Undivided Trinity - one of his favourites. In later years this was again changed and is now The Holy Trinity, SS Peter and Paul with St. Swithin.

The manor of Elyndon was in 844 A.D. recorded as owned by the Abbey of Malmesbury, but was willed to the Abbey of Winchester in 974 A.D. The monies from the Elyndon manor were to provide for the support of the monks of the Priory of St. Swithin and it is this connection which gave rise to the name of Prior's Hill, part of the estate. The Domesday survey of 1086 still records the manor as belonging to Winchester Abbey. At about this time it seems the old, probably wooden Saxon-building was destroyed and replaced by a Norman stone building, fragments of which may still be seen. After the Dissolution of the Monastries in 1541 the manor devolved to the dean and Chapter of Winchester Cathedral and patronage of the Benefice to the Bishop of Winchester. The question of the legitimate patronage had been raised more than once and the varying patrons recorded as presenting minsters does appear confusing. However, we find in the Register of John of Pontissara the claim that the Church having been founded by the Crown, the patronage should lie with the Crown. By 1296 however the same Bishop's register notes that the Church of Elyndon is one of those of which the Bishop of Winchester (perhaps as successor to the Abbott to whom the manor had been bequeathed) is patron though lying within the diocese of Salisbury. This meant that should a vacancy occur at a time when the Winchester See was also vacant, the King might make the presentation of the Rector. The Rector was in his turn the usual person to present the vicar, but in the former's absence the diocesan Bishop would undertake the task.

In 1826 new Diocesan boundaries were drawn and Wroughton was transferred to the Diocese of Gloucester and Bristol. Later still, at the turn of the century, it passed to Bristol alone.

The form of worship in the earliest times will have been the Celtic Catholic form, subsequently following the Roman form after the agreement of this at the Synod of Whitby in 644 A.D. until the Reformation. During the mid sixteenth century the rite would have been observed as seemed most expedient according to the monarch of the day, the Anglican rite becoming the rule early in the reign of Elizabeth I (1558 - 1603). This uncertainty is to some degree reflected in the changes in the ministry of the period.

The parish income devolved initially from tithes, part of which supported the monks as we have already noted and, in 1172 a charter of Bishop Henry de Blois confirms this to the Monks of St. Swithin together with a comment "And the church of Elyndone for the writing of books and repairing of organs". We know from exact records (Taxatio 1293) that in the late 13th century the total income of the parish was 67 marks (about £44.66) of which the monks received 35 marks and the vicar 6½.

The acreage of the whole Parish in 1956 was 6,950 and this accords quite well with the measurements given in the Domesday survey. By 1678 the lands from which the Rectory income came were about 120 acres and the Vicarage about 1½ acres. The rectors land was let and the rent partly payable to the Vicar. Elcombe Manor had been owned for more than two hundred years by the Lovel family who also had estates in France at Ivry, hence the derivative name Ivery for land around the old Vicarage. Part of the tithe from this estate went to the support of monks at Ivry.

2. The Parish Church in 1846

3. The Parish Church today

4. Wesleyan Chapel, Devizes Road. Demolished to make way for the community centre surroundings. (Wilts. Newspapers)

5. The Methodist Chapel, completed in 1880

After the Ecclesiastical Commission of 1836 the Rectory was to lapse with the death of the Rector and in 1866 with the death of Richard Pretyman the income therefore became part of the Common Fund of the Ecclesiastical Commissioners. The manor property also came into their hands at this time. The Rectory had been let since 1781 to the Codrington family. Subsequently they were able to buy the property and it remains in their ownership to the present day. The manor of Elcombe had been confiscated by the crown on the attainder of the last Lord Lovel and subsequently given by Henry VIII to Sir William Compton. His grandson later sold the property to Thomas Sutton, founder of the Charterhouse. The income from the Rectory lands now being paid directly to the Commissioners, they assumed responsibility for the upkeep of the Chancel of the Church and the Parishioners were left with responsibility for the remainder.

St. Mary, Elcombe, in the Parish of Elyndon

The Lovel family who owned the Manor of Elcombe as already noted, maintained their own chantry chapel close to their house. Its date of foundation is not known. The family certainly had the Manor as early as 1127 when there is a record of money being paid to Ivry Abbey from the Elcombe tithe. In 1308 the Register of Simon of Ghent, Bishop of Salisbury refers to the "Vacant chapel of Ellacombe" from which one infers a foundation earlier than this. At this time Roger Grymbaud was presented by the Lord John Lovel, soldier, at Ramsbury to be inducted Priest to the Chapel.

The latest recorded presentation of a Priest for the Chapel was in 1448. At some unknown date the Chapel was finally demolished and today its exact site is uncertain though it is said some of the stone is incorporated in the walls of Legge House which was built as a School. The font was preserved and for many years lay idle in the Baptistry of the Parish Church. Since 1979 it has however been restored to use, replacing the more modern one which was transferred to another church.

St. Joseph's

The Catholic faith was always followed by a minority even after the Reformation, and in the early twentieth century several Roman Catholic families from the village are represented as members of Holy Rood, Swindon. Monsignor Pitt tells that they "Enjoyed the bracing walk" each Sunday. The Catholics built a Church Hall and dedicated it in 1953. It was then decided to retain this as the Church - the St. Joseph's we know today and a Catholic Parish in its own right. Nearby on the site of the old Barcelona House now stands the Convent of the Holy Spirit, home for a German Order of Nuns.

The Methodist Church

The Methodist's have the distinction of being the first Non-conformist Church to have a permanent building in the village. Precise dates are difficult to find, even from Central Hall records. The first Primitive Methodist Chapel was at lower Overtown close to the site of the present Convent. In 1853 another was built in the High Street and is now seen converted into two houses. Yet another, the Wesleyan, in Devizes Road, was demolished to make way for the Community Centre.

The building now in use in the High Street was completed in 1880 its foundation stones having been laid in September 1879 by Messrs T Harris of Calne, S Humphries of Noremarsh, I Humphries of Broad Hinton, L L Morse and M Trotman of Stratton and Mrs Deacon of Blunsdon. The cost of the building was an estimated £520! In 1904 Schoolroom buildings were added at a cost of £495. The movement has always been involved in village life and the Wroughton Silver Band was originally founded in 1900 as the Wroughton Primitive Methodist Band. In its early days it assembled on Sunday mornings at either the Swan Inn, Brimble Hill or Wharf Road before marching to the Chapel for the Service. Even though the membership of the Band became wider after the second World War the Band continued to use the Methodist Schoolroom as their base until 1978 when the new Band Room at Burderop was made available.

The Baptist Church

The Baptists no longer meet in the village though for a few years from 1902 - 1912 they met in the old Ellendune Hall, demolished a few years ago and now the site of the War Memorial. They also held Sunday evening meetings outside the Swan. However, lack of funds meant that the endeavour ended and the few Baptists in the village are of course now incorporated in the United Reformed Church in Swindon.

In 1576 a census records that of 260 souls, in the village, but one was non-conformist. Today the population exceeds 8000. About 240 adults are registered members of the Church of England with the Catholics and Methodists numbering up to 100 adults each. However, infrequently people use the Church buildings today there are very few who when questioned deny adherence to one of the Churches and the three major Churches in the village work together as closely as possible with some sharing of activities and in particular it is their active joint participation which produces the village Magazine, the Wroughton Monthly. The Wroughton Council of Churches was formed to promote such co-operation in the village.

This account of the History of the Church in Wroughton is necessarily incomplete. Research is considerably hindered by lack of time and especially by the loss of old Salisbury Diocesan records following a fire at their Archives some years ago. Hopefully further information will be available in time for our second edition!

References and Sources of Information

The Early Charters of Wessex. H.P.R. Finberg 1964
Diocesan Records at Winchester
Early annals of the Episcopate in Wilts & Dorset. W.H. Jones 1871.
W.A. Magasines
A Visitor's Guide to the Parish Church
St John the Baptist and St Helen, Wroughton   M.Child 1978

Table 1

Rectors of Wroughton

       The appointment was commonly a sinecure, a Vicar being appointed to the cure or care of souls.

Year	Rector	Notes
1239	*Accession of Edward I*	
1250	Peter de Abusun	a kinsman of the King
1260	John de Wyham	King's chaplain
1281	Solomon de Roffa	
1282	Nicholaus de Pechane	
1303	Robert de Harewedon	Presented by the Bishop of Winchester
		King's Justice – resigned 14th Jan 1304
1304	Theobald de Threngden	Abbot of Hyde – Presented by the King the see of Winchester being vacant
1307	*Accession of Edward II*	
1316	Richard de Lustehalle	Presented by the King
1327	*Accession of Edward III*	Collated to the Mastership of
1338	*Hundred Years War began*	St Cross Hospital
1346	*Battle of Crecy*	by Bishop Edyndon
1349	John de Wavelegh or Woversey of Netheravon	
1349	Roger Helm	
1349	Thomas de Beauford	
1349/50	James de Beauford – resigned 1354	
1354	Thomas de Beauford	
1356	*Battle of Poitiers*	
1357	Nicholas de Kaerwent	King's Clerk – resigned 1361
1361	Thomas Yonge	became Archdeacon of Worcester
1361	John Blaunchard	Doctor of Law
1371	Simon Clement	
1379/80	John de Gurminchestre	Exchange with Simon Clement
1381	*The Peasants Revolt*	Prebend of North Alton, Sarum Cathedral
1387	Thomas Lavington	became Prebend of Exeter Cathedral 1394
1388	John Mason als Spicer	exchange with Thomas Lavington "if found not to sing Latin well he is to have an office without cure only".
1389	John Ware	
1405	Robert Burgeys	
1408	John Giles	1414 received Papel dispensation enabling him to hold benefice's and receive promotion despite his illegitimacy
1413	*Accession of Henry V*	
1415	*Battle of Agincourt*	
1416	William Thame	
1434	William Pentriche	
1446	John Stradlying	to Llandaff 1448
1448	Robert Cole	from Llandaff
1453	*End of Hundred Years War*	
1472	David Husband	
1485	*Accession of Henry VII having defeated Richard III at Battle of Bosworth*	
1491	Adrian de Bard	a Florentine he was also Rector of St Peters', Marlborough 1483 – 1486
1493	Randolph Hethcote	Also a former Rector of St Peter's Marlborough 1481 – 1483. Perhaps Wroughton was promotion?
1496	Edmund Chaderton or Chatterton died 1499	

1499 Christopher Bainbridge

1508 Archbishop of York
1511 Cardinal
A north countryman he was educated at Queens College, Oxford. Before becoming Archbishop he was both Provost and Dean of York and in 1505 Dean of Windsor when he also became Master of the Rolls - a predecessor of Lord Denning today. A favourite of Henry VIII he died in Rome 14.7.1514 having been poisoned.

1506 Richard Gardiner
1509 Accession of Henry VIII
1519 John Foxe
1530 Anthony Barker
1547 Accession of Edward VI
1551 Edward Gascoyn
1551 Richard Martindale

Appointment invalidated
Pensioner of Kings College deprived 1559

1553 Accession of Mary I
1558 Accession of Elizabeth I
1560 Griffith Williams

Presented by the Queen Elizabeth on the deprivation of Martindale.
became Bishop of Worcester 1580
buried in the Cathedral

1573 John Watson

Public Orator 1559. MP for Hindon member of Archbishop Parker's Household he assisted him in literary work. He lost his preferments for "irregularity of conduct" but nevertheless became master of Faculties and Judge of the Prerogative Court Dublin 1577

1575 George Ackworth

Presented by Queen Elizabeth I

1580 Anthony Pepper
Hiatus in Episcopal Register 1584/8
1596 Philip Bisse
1603 Accession of James I
1610 Thomas Bisse
1632 Walter Raleigh

son of Richard of Stokeland, Somerset

Presented by the King
Son of Sir Carew Raleigh of Downton, and nephew of Sir Water Raleigh. Loyal to Charles I he was persecuted at the outbreak of Civil War. Taken prisoner at Bridgewater in July 1645 he was placed under house arrest in Wells in the custody of a shoemaker who ill-treated him and in a quarrel injured him with a sword. He died from his injury in October 1646 and was buried in the Choir of Wells Cathedral.

1642 Civil War

1646 Thomas Stubbs

1649 Execution of Charles I

Was vicar at the time but granted the Rectory when it was sequested from Raleigh for "delinquency" in 1658 he himself was reprimanded by the Chairman of the Commissioners for brawling and quarrelling with his neighbours and reviling professors of godliness. At the restoration he remained Vicar, but did not retain the rectory.
Resigned 1679

1660 Robert Newlin

1679 Francis Morley   Probably grandson of Bishop George
                                         Morley. Claimed title of Prebend
                                         of Elingdon als Wroughton in
                                         Ecclesia St. Swithin de Winton
1696 Edward Jones   Donor of Communion Plate 1719
1714 Accession of George I
1736 John Headley   Youngest son of Bishop Samuel Headley
                                         Poet and Dramatist. His notoriety
                                         equalled that of his father.

1743 John Conart
1779 Edmund Ferrers   Barrister-at-law - Inner Temple
                                         In 1807 granted the lease of
                                         Wroughton Rectory,
1783 Pitt the Younger appointed   To Mary Codrington, widow, Sir Isaac
Prime Minister, aged 24   Pocock and Rev John Prower as
                                         executors of the will of William
                                         Codrington at a yearly rent of £50
                                         and £45 to the Vicar.
1825/1866 Richard Pretyman   Youngest son of Bishop George Pretyman
                                         Tomlin of Winchester who was tutor to
                                         Pitt. On his death the rectory passed
                                         into the hands of the Ecclesiastical
                                         Commissioners.

1848 French Revolution
1863 Battle of Gettysburg

Table 2

Vicars of Elyndon als Wroughton

1316 William de Leycester   Presented by Lord Bishop of Salisbury.
                                         Not only was the See of Winchester
                                         vacant but so too was the Rectory at
                                         the time of the death of the last
                                         Vicar, whose identity is unknown.
1324 Richard Lambert   Presented by Rector Richard de Lustehulle
1325 John de Gravele   Presented by Rector
1354/1361 Hiatus in Epuscopal Register
  - John Hayles   Presented by Rector
1361 John de Baa als Eweln   Presented by Rector
1387 Walter Persoun   Presented by Rector
1389 John Bridport   Presented by Bishop of Winchester
1405 Nicholas Burgh   Vicar by Exchange
1428 John Sconar   Vicar by Exchange
1438 John Trent
1439 John Honeyland   was charged for assault on several
                                         people at Hornblowton in Somerset,
                                         theft of 3s 4d (about 17 pence) from
                                         one of them, John Brown and for
                                         having broken into the Church of
                                         Elyndon and taken various goods and
                                         money from it on the Thursday after
                                         the feast of St Leonard. He was
                                         however pardoned of all these charges.
1449   John Benger   Presented by Rector
1491   Matthew Foxe   Presented by Bishop of Salisbury
1449/1502 Hiatus in Episcopal Register
1535 George Banks   Presented by Rector

1545 Richard Hode	Presented by Rector
1545 James Hall	" " "
1570 John Angell	" " "
1577 John Pettie	Also Rector of Lydiard Tregoze 1576/1612
1612 Oliver Brunsell	Tobias Crisp, Rector of Brinkworth, preached a laudatory sermon at his funeral.
1641 Thomas Stubbs	Also Rector during the Commonwealth Buried at Wroughton 24th April 1666
1666 Thomas Newlin	
1682 John Brackley	
1716 Thomas Saddler	Son of Robert Saddler of Elcombe Many Saddler family monuments are in the Church. The Vicarage, now Ivery House, was rebuilt at this time and a date stone of 1727 is seen in its wall. Buried at Wroughton 9th May 1755
1755 John Descrambes	Buried at Wroughton 22nd July 1777
1778 Francis Porter	Presented by Bishop of Salisbury Buried at Wroughton 28th March 1782
1782 John Bromfield Ferrers	
1783 James Merest	In 1812 noted by Rural Dean to be keeping a school at Diss, Norfolk.
1827 Thomas Stretton Codrington	Son of William Buried at Wroughton 12th December 1839
1840 Henry William Maurice Light	Gave the present pulpit in 1852, also Lecturn and Bible. Buried at Wroughton 2nd April 1875
1875 John Richard Turner	Presented by Bishop of Gloucester and Bristol Buried at Wroughton 13th February 1908 aged 83
1908 Richard James Keble	Presented by Bishop of Bristol
1911 Archibald Charles Clark-Kennedy	
1926 Gilbert Hankey	His brother William Lee Hankey painted the Christ and twelve apostles in the sixteenth century stone reredos of the south aisle Chapel.
1941 Eric Vivian Rees	Became an Honorary Canon of Bristol Cathedral.
1956 John Capenhurst Burnett	Became an Honorary Canon of Bristol Cathedral. Transferred to a Bristol Parish in 1976. His wife had been a teacher at the Infants School.
1976 Ronald George Wolsey	Became an Honorary Canon of Bristol Cathedral. Retired 1980 to Wootton Bassett.
1981 Ronald Lucas	Presented by the Bishop of Bristol Previously at Park, Swindon.

Table 3

Priests of the Chapel of St Mary, Elcombe in the Parish of Elyndon

Year	Priest	Presented by
1308	Roger Grymbaud	Presented by Sir John Lovel
1381	John de la Mare	Presented by Johanna, wife of Lord Lovel
1319	Geoffrey de Mersten	Presented by Johanna, wife of Lord Lovel
1329	Thames le Templan	" " " " " " "
1346	Simon de Broc	" " " " " " "
1349	John Palmer de Shulton	Presented by Bishop of Salisbury
1361	Walter de Keepe	Presented by the King for the heirs of John Lovel
1362	Peter Grey	Presented by the Bishop of Salisbury
1419	John Whitmore	Presented by Matilda, Lady Lovel and Holand
1435	John Potter	Presented by William, Lord Lovel and Holand
1448	John de Rew	Presented by William, Lord Lovel and Holand

6. Ivery house 'loft school'

INFANTS SCHOOL WROUGHTON

7. Infant school 1874-1928. Now the Church Hall

EDUCATION

by

John Gibbs

In the garden of the old rectory house (now Ivery House) stands an old stable building which was once used as a school. The upstairs room was for girls, and downstairs, called the 'abbey kitchen,' was for boys. The money to pay for this school, and another at Broad Hinton, was provided by Thomas Benet of Salthrop, who on June 2nd 1749 put a charge on his manor of Quidhampton to provide £40 per annum, to be divided equally between the two schoolmasters. They were to teach the poor children of the Parish, aged between five and sixteen, to read, write and do arithmetic. They also had to instruct the children in the catechism and true principles and doctrine of the Church of England, which was further helped by taking the children to church twice on Sundays.

The number of scholars at the Wroughton School was limited to thirty-six, but in 1818 it was incorporated into the National Society, opening it to all the Parish. According to the "Report of Select Committee on the Education of the Lower Orders 1819", there were two hundred children, and the teacher received £35 per annum, house-rent and firing, which was made up by subscription. The same report mentions the existence of a Boarding School and makes the Observation:-

"The poor are thankful for the means of instruction afforded them".

By 1859 the school was reported to be in poor condition and was eventually replaced in 1867 by the building now known as Legge House. It is said that stone from the Chapel at Elcombe was used to build the new school.

The School quickly became overcrowded and a new school was built for infants. This opened in September 1874 and remained in use until 1928. It is still a familiar building in the village - the Church Hall. It is difficult to imagine how either teachers or pupils survived the conditions in that school. In the winter of 1914 classroom temperatures were down in the 30s and one log book entry reads:-

"The small fire in the large room had to be put out at nine o'clock this morning. The smoke was so bad that it was impossible to keep the fire in. The schoolroom was full of smoke and it was some time before we could get the fire properly out and the room clear of smoke."

The number of pupils varied between about 100 and 150 with a staff of four. During one week in November 1917, the average attendance was 115 and there were only two teachers. On the 7th December that year they were pleased to report, "A kettle was received today to provide hot water for making the dinner children cocoa to drink."

Over the years there were many serious epidemics of whooping cough and measles, requiring the school to be closed for several weeks at a time.

On January 7th 1929 the infants started in a new building which is still part of the present Infants' School. Additional buildings have been erected around that original school (the part with the veranda) including temporary prefabricated classrooms.

Legge house continued as a mixed school until 1880, when a new building was erected for girls. The new building is in use today, by the Infants', and is that part situated on the west side of School Lane. The girls' school opened on August 23rd 1880 and an early entry in the log book reads:-

"School opened. 106 children admitted. Cautioned children r specting marking on walls".

Legge House was formally established as the Upper Wroughton School in 1885 and in 1906 the title was extended to the Upper Wroughton Church of England School. In January 1929 it was re-organised as a co-educational establishment. In 1948, owing to cramped conditions, a hutted camp built during the war at Burderop Park was opened as a Secondary Modern school until new premises could be built. Legge House was closed, but re-opened in September 1950 because of increased numbers attending the Junior School.

There are several references to a Private School in Wroughton. Whether these all refer to the same one is not clear. The North Wilts Directory of 1890 has an entry:-
"Mrs Butler - ladies and gentlemens private school. Belgrave House". However in 1895 and 1901 the same directory lists:-
"Butler, Miss E - private school High Street".
Is this coincidence, were they related, or is it possibly an error? There are two references to Miss Butler's school in the Infants' School Log Books:-
March 7th 1917 "...... The heating of the school seriously needs attention. Several children have been ill - their parents say through sitting in draughts and two or three have left and attend Miss Butler's school through the unhealthy conditions of the school."

September 15th 1919. "During the last few days 6 new children have been admitted, each about 6½ yrs. of age from Miss Butler's School. They are very backward indeed and have to be placed in Class 11."

Although the 1870 Education Act offered education to all, many of the poorer families in Wroughton sent their children to school only intermittently or not at all, as every penny counted in feeding large families on excessively low wages. Take for example the family of John Shand and his wife Hannah who lived in Hay Lane in 1871. They had seven children between the ages of two and twenty. John and his two elder sons, William, 15, and John, 11, were low-paid agricultural labourers, wife Hannah and daughter Sarah took in laundry. Only Charles, 9, Laura, 7, and James, 4, were listed as attending school (Willie at 2 was too young). They shared their cottage with four other people. You can imagine the scene on a winter morning as the tree children struggled from straw mattresses in an unheated loft to wash their face and hands under the icy pump in the back yard, whilst the adults plodded off to long cold days on the land, inadequately clothed and fed. Breakfast for the children would be ale and bread for Charles, and milk and bread for Laura and James. Boots and coats or shawls would be donned, little packets of bread and cheese hastily packed, and the cold walk across the fields to school begun. This would take them below Salthrop House, where their wealthy employers lived in luxury, into Elcombe Street, then through the cottages past Elcombe House to the footpath up to the Church and new school. Straggly groups of children would appear along muddy tracks and from dark cottage doorways to swell the throng. As they reached the top of the hill the clanging of a bell would signify that it was time to line up and file into the chilly, smoky rooms for the day's lessons to begin.

First would be assembly with the partitions pulled back and stern-looking teachers ranged in front. Then a hymn, a prayer and a reading from the Bible, followed by boot and head inspections and the dispatching home of those not up to standard. Recitation of the catechism in class followed, and the admonition of those who did not know it, then English and Maths. It was said that such children should be taught and instructed to read perfectly their mother tongue, to write a good plain and fair handwriting in the Roman character and to cast accounts.

8. Miss Butler's private school with Miss Emily in charge

9. The Girls School, School Lane. Now part of the Infants'

10. Legge House, near the Church

11. The inscription on Legge House

12. A mixed class in 1913

13. A boys class of unknown date

During the day the children took it in turns to sit near the coke stove as it was so cold in the outer reaches of the room. At lunch time the children would huddle round the stove to eat their bread and cheese, and water would be heated on the stove for a hot drink. Each day included a short P.E. lesson in which the children stood fully clothed in straight lines on the playground and copied exercises in unison. School finished early in winter time to allow children to reach home before dark, so Charles, Laura and James would skip off down the hill to enjoy a little freedom before they reached home and the ceaseless round of chores began.

Most labourers' children were forced to leave school at the age of ten or eleven years to earn money. Hay Lane seems to have been particularly poor with a number of young children working, for example, Henry James Beasom, 10, plough boy living away from home and Robert Morse, 10, labouring at home.

This picture of life a century ago contrasts strongly with today's centrally heated buildings, metalled roads and motorised transport. During the 1960s the village grew rapidly, and with this expansion came the new Junior School in 1965, followed by Ridgeway Comprehensive two years later.

References and Sources of Information

Census Returns 1841-1871
Surviving School Log Books
These will provide enough material for a Study in a future volume.

THE HEALTH AND POOR LAW OF THE VILLAGE OF WROUGHTON

by

Hilary Dunscombe

Someone once said, "There is nothing new on the face of the earth" ideas and attempts at solutions may change but the same basic problems continue and are met by each generation as if they have never before existed. The problems faced by the poor and sick in Wroughton are similar to those of every village community in this part of England, but small pieces of very intimate information about people and the locality help to make the story unique.

The history of Wroughton fades back into the time of the building of Ellandune on the hill and around the Church but written evidence which can tell us about the lives of the people of the parish is only available from the time of the Norman Conquest in 1066. For several hundred years the Manorial system existed in the parish with separate Manors at Wertune, Wervetone, Salteharpe, Ellendune and Elcombe each responsible for the welfare of their own employees. The Manor of Ellendune at the foot of Prior's Hill was, up to the time of the Dissolution of the monasteries, owned by monks from the Bishopric of Winchester. Poor children before the sixteenth century had little chance of breaking free from the Manorial system with all its restrictions, and spent most of their lives within the Parish of their birth, their only chance of education being the goodwill of the Parish Priest or local monks who would voluntarily spend time teaching the basics of religion, reading and arithmetic. Life expectancy at this time was very low, although a few survived to old age. Leprosy was quite an accepted thing in the area, with centres for treatment being set up by the church in Malmesbury and Marlborough in the fourteenth and fifteenth centuries. There is no written evidence of the Plague in Wroughton, but it certainly came to the county in the sixteenth and seventeenth centuries, and fear of it must have sent its ripples amongst the inhabitants of Wroughton.

When Henry VIII set in motion the Dissolution of the Monasteries in the 1530's, little thought had been given to the social implications of such a move, and Wroughton, like every other village and town, was left with the problems of caring for the chronically sick, isolating those suffering from infectious diseases and feeding the vast numbers of unemployed who had once worked on church lands. For more than forty years the problems of the poor and sick were virtually ignored and it was left to the goodwill of Parishes or individuals to do what they thought best. By the end of the sixteenth century the situation was desperate, with armed bands of poor and homeless wandering the countryside stealing sometimes for gain but usually just to keep body and soul together.

It was in 1601 in the last years of the reign of Queen Elizabeth I that "An Act for the Relief of the Poor" was passed and that Wroughton posted on the door of the Church the names of its first two Overseers of the Poor who, together with the Church Wardens, were to be responsible for the poor and needy of the Parish. The names of the two overseers have been lost, but they must have been substantial householders and residents of the parish of Wroughton. Before taking office they had to appear before two county Justices of the Peace and swear to carry out their duties honestly and keep records of all monetry transactions.

During the first year the poor of the parish were registered officially, and any not born within the parish were sent back to their place of birth. Many returned home to Wroughton after years of wandering, secure in the knowledge that at least they would not die of starvation or cold.

The seventeenth century is one of darkness as far as written evidence is concerned, but it is possible that accounts and certificates were kept but have been lost during the passage of time. It was certainly a century during which the movement of the poor was restricted, but the Civil War and new religious ideas must have added to the unrest and ambitions of the poor.

By the eighteenth century, a system for the organisation of the poor was evolving fast and massive amounts of paper work were overtaking the Church Wardens and Overseers of the Poor which limited those able to undertake the work to the definitely literate members of the parish. "Rules governing Overseers of the Poor" were very detailed by the mid eighteenth century, and penalties for deliberate deceit or carelessness severe.

The poor had become the responsibility of the whole parish, and every move the Overseer made had to be made public on the Church door. Once every month, on a Sunday afternoon, the Wroughton Overseers met in the vestry of the parish curch to discuss the problems of the previous month. Each month adults and children were discussed who had no means of supporting themselves. Each village had a main trade developed by the Overseers in which the unemployed could be found work. In Wroughton this was the wool trade, as many sheep were kept in the area and the raw materials were readily available. The centre of the trade was the Workhouse which was situated at the bottom of Markham Road where Pavy Cottages now stand. (plate 14). It was only intended that about thirty people should actually live in, these were called "Indoor Paupers" and usually there was a high proportion of children who were orphaned or illegitimate. The "Outdoor Paupers", about 200 of them, lived in poor law cottages built on old common land, but were often employed in the wool trade when other work was not available. The Victorian equivalent of these cottages can be seen on the left hand side of the High Street as you climb the steeper part of the hill towards the church. The wool appears to have been cleaned and carded, but there is no evidence of completed articles made of wool. In the lists of traders in the village at various dates there is no reference to weavers, so the wool must have been sent elsewhere.

The basic essentials of life were provided at the Workhouse but life was hard. Each registered pauper was allocated a bedstead on which was a cover stuffed with feathers, flock (wool, cotton, hair and other odds and ends) or chaff. Two wool blankets and a coverlet were provided in most rooms, although one room appeared to provide only one blanket per bed. Bolsters and bolster cases were provided, and each person had their own bedside mat. Most of the sleeping accommodation was in the "garrets" over the main rooms of the workhouse. Most "garrets" had a table and a couple of chairs and an odd assortment of chests and boxes for the storage of people's meagre personal possessions. The main room and the largest was the Workhouse itself in which the work was done for long hours each day. It contained two long wooden tables, seven forms and seven pairs of "carding stock" and a "cardstack" used for preparing the wool. Two books obligatory to all Workhouses stood on a shelf: "The Whole Duty of Man" and a "Bible" from which the Overseers

14. The Workhouse Cottages which used to stand at the lower end of Markham Road, then called Workhouse Road

were supposed to read to the paupers at regular intervals for the good of their souls. When a person was first accepted to live at the Workhouse they were supplied with a decent suit and old clothes for working. The rule of the Workhouse was that "All goods were to be left in as good a condition as found".

The bakehouse too must have been fairly large according to the inventory made in 1789. It contained three separate furnaces for baking, as well as seven storage tubs and a dough trough (probably wooden) for the mixing of the bread which formed the main part of the diet of the poor at this time. Other things listed were a carving knife, peeler, fork, one long table, two benches, a small brass pot, a little iron pot, a pail, a ladle, a hand bowl, an iron bowl, a strainer, three buckets, a hoke, three wooden dishes, a lye and a dropper. Food was served at the long well scrubbed wooden tables in the Workhouse. It was served on wooden trenchers with the name of the Workhouse marked on the back (Some of these from Stratton Workhouse are preserved at Swindon Museum). Wooden spoons were provided, but most people owned a pocket knife and used this to cut up food. Ale locally brewed was drunk from cans made of tin ware.

When for some reason a person became unfit for work, he or she was the responsibility of their home parish, and, if working in another parish, was legally required to return to Wroughton to be cared for by relations, often with financial assistance from the Overseers of the poor or to be cared for in the Workhouse.

The money for the upkeep of the poor was raised in several ways, but by far the largest amount came from the poor rate. This was a rate levied on the parish annually, although in the years 1770-74 double rates had to be levied in the village to cover the extra costs of equipping the Workhouse. Everyone who owned property was reassessed annually and the amounts required announced in church and displayed on the church door. Many people were so poor that they could not possibly pay the amount required, and they could appeal to the Overseers for rate relief. This would be discussed at the next Vestry and each case carefully studied and a decision made. Lists of those excused payment are still in existence. In all places the poor rate was a very heavy burden, and often money had to be borrowed from elsewhere. Some of these debts were never cleared, and were just written off in late Victorian times.

Wroughton was fortunate to have three benefactors who lifted a little of the burden by investing money towards various charities in the village.

The owner of the Manor House at Salthrop in 1743, Thomas Benet Esquire, allocated £20 per annum (to be paid quarterly) from the profits of his farm at Quidhampton, and also the interest of £300 at 3½% per annum to be paid out of his farm called Constable at Broadhinton for the setting up of a charity school in the Wroughton Parish for poor children of the Wroughton and Broad Hinton parishes. The school was established in a loft over the stable at the Vicarage (Ivery House) and a fee of 2d per week was charged. It was mainly the industrious poor who took advantage of this opportunity. Most children stayed four or five years until they were old enough to work with their parents. Until 1817 all the teaching was done by the clergymen who were restricted by law to teach "only the Christian Religion as established by the Church of England, reading and writing of the English tongue and common Arithmetic" (not to be used for teaching any other language or science).

Mr Thomas Benet's sister Elizabeth Benet who lived in Wroughton gave the interest on £200 at 3½% per annum from the farm of Constables at Broad Hinton for the use of poor girls of the Parish to provide them with a new outfit of clothes after twelve months of responsible service with their first employer. Most girls in the village went into service in the surrounding towns and villages until they married, as it was almost the only way a young girl could earn money. Hiring fairs were held in the High Street in Swindon every Spring and Autumn, and girls went there to meet and discuss terms with prospective employers from the surrounding areas. On an average about thirteen girls a year from the parish of Wroughton entered service. (see plate 16b). Boys too went to the fairs seeking agricultural work. The early letters of application for the ten shilling allowance have been lost, but the Victorian ones remain. Here is an example.

Lydiard Millicent
1868

Sir,

This is to certify that Ellen Simpkins, the daughter of Job Simpkins of the Parish of Wroughton, is living as servant to Mr Robert Horton of Lydiard Millicent. She at present suits her Master very well and is engaged to stay with him for the twelve months.

Yours truly,

Robert Horton.

Mr Thomas Benet, his wife and his sister Elizabeth all gave twenty pounds at their deaths to be distributed among the poor as required. The Benets were an influential and wealthy family, Mrs Benet's uncle being the Right Honourable John Smith of South Todworth, Hants., Speaker of the House of Commons and Chancellor of the Exchequer in the reign of Queen Anne. On her memorial in Wroughton Church it says "The beauties of her person were great but much exceeded by y virtues of her mind. She was constant in her devotions towards God and charities to y poor as well, knowing prayer without alms are of little value".

Another family noted for their charity were the Sadlers but the only recorded ongoing charity was that given by Mrs Jane Bendry. On her memorial in the Church it says "She gave upwards of two thousand pounds to her indigent friends and relations during the last two years of her life, and among the many legacies she left at her death was twenty pounds per annum to the poor of this parish to be paid by her executive for twenty years". Dated November 28th 1775 and completed by this quotation "He that giveth to the poor lendeth to the Lord. Go and do thou likewise."

Mr Bendry, another considerable landowner in the village, gave £8 per annum from his estate (which was behind the High Street on the south side) for the apprenticing of poor boys in the parish. Wroughton appears to have been a flourishing community with many trades connected with the horse racing fraternity in the later eighteenth century, so openings were available for apprentice saddlers, blacksmiths and harness makers. Other trades were bakers, millers, carpenters, carriers, shoemakers, butchers, beer retailers, drapers, grocers, maltsters, wheelers and bacon factors. These were encouraged to take on poor boys as apprentices as often as possible to ease the strain on the poor rate. Boys were required to remain at their apprenticeship until their twentyfirst birthday. Girls could only leave when they married. Any person who left a job or a house rented from the parish because they didn't like it could expect no more relief from the parish for the rest of their life.

One of the greatest burdens on the parish were illegitimate children, many of whom spent their whole childhood in the workhouse because no one would employ their mothers. Attitudes to this were very rigid and the mother and child were social outcasts. To get maintenance for herself and her child, the mother had to go before the magistrates to swear to the identity of the father. The choice was simple - tell his name or starve. He then was enfor:ed by law to pay to the Poor Law Union an agreed annual amount for the upkeep of the child. From 1760 onwards lists were kept in Wroughton with a steady average of about three illegitimate children a year. Women's names tend to appear more than once, men's rarely more than once - they probably couldn't afford it.

Although to the pauper the Parish Overseers must have seemed the ultimate authority, Wroughton was only a tiny dot in a nationwide network of rules, regulations and never ending paperwork. The local overseers' immediate superiors were "The Highworth and Swindon Poor Law Union" (Highworth first because at this time it was a larger more thriving town than Swindon). Meetings of the officials took place at the end of the century in the "Goddard Arms" in Swindon, as it was central to an administrative area covering roughly the present Thamesdown. This Union was responsible for numerous parishes and evidences for workhouses at Highworth, Stratton, Purton and Swindon, as well as Wroughton, still exists. Every certificate issued had to be signed by Justices of the Peace who paid regular visits to the "Goddard Arms", and many very frightened illiterate Wroughtonians must have been marched by the village constable up the hill to Swindon to swear on oath and sign a shaky signature or scratch a distinctive cross on long wordy certificates covered in signatures and personal seals. This Union was responsible to the Wilts. and Berks. County Council who in turn had to send in reports to the Government.

Until the 1780's all certificates issued were hand written by the local overseers or a clerk, but followed exact wording supplied by the Government. It must have been a great timesaver when the printed forms first appeared in 1783 and there were only odd details to be filled in. Large numbers of these certificates still exist in the County Record Office.

It was possible for a pauper to move to another parish if they were properly registered and held a certificate. On arrival they had to go before the local magistrates and give a sworn statement of identity which was sent by carrier to Wroughton. If Wroughton did not send a confirmation of this statement within twentyone days the pauper had to return home and again draw poor-rate in the village. Some paupers made very long journeys considering their lack of money in attempts to make a better life elsewhere. Certificates exist for as far afield as St. Helen's in Lancashire, Welsh Newton in Monmouthshire and Princes Risborough. Whilst some moved out others were moving in. For example this hand written certificate was received in 1752:

"John Winkworth, Thomas Chubb, John Taylor and Olive Mills,
Church Wardens and Overseers of the Poor of the Parish of Wantage
in the County of Berks, aforesaid do own and acknowledge
John Freaker and Martha his wife and Mary their daughter (about
two years of age) to be our inhabitants legally settled in the
Parish of Wantage in the County of Berks aforesaid. In witness
whereof we have hereunto set our hands this second day of June
in the Twentyfifth year of the Reign of our Sovereign Lord George
the Second by the Grace of God of Great Britain, France and
Ireland, King Defender of the Faith and in the Year of Our Lord
one thousand seven hundred and fiftytwo".

This family was legally accepted into the village and paid the poor-rate
as long as was necessary.

Another drain on the poor-rate was the payments made to men
serving in the Wilts and Sarum division of the Militia. Each parish had
to supply a certain number of men annually and pay half their wages plus
any money needed to support their families whilst they were away.
It was quite possible to find a substitute if men didn't wish to go,
and often the poor would jump at the opportunity of regular money.
In 1798 George Miles a carpenter was chosen by lot but was able to
persuade James Phillips to substitute for him, and a long complicated
"Militia Certificate" was issued. Some men preferred to have their
families with them during service, and they presented their certificates
and claimed their money wherever they were stationed. The money was
then claimed back from Wroughton.

At this time a piece of land was owned by the Poor Law Union
approximately where the shopping centre now stands and the profits from
this went towards the Poor Rate.

Healthwise this was still a time of uncertainty. Leprosy and
Plague had gone for good but several other kinds of epidemics were still
common, mainly smallpox and fever. To deal with these emergencies a
Pest House built of brick and stone stood on the hill south of the
present Co-op building. The spot can still be identified by a rough
triangle of hedges and uneven ground, although the building has disappeared. To this place were sent all people who developed dangerously
infectious diseases, until they recovered or died. No-one was allowed
to visit and provisions were left on the village side of the stream to
be collected. A special right of way was made from the Pest House to
the stream so that there was no fear of accidental meetings. Often
whole families would have caught the disease before it was diagnosed
and sad lists of deaths appear close together in the Parish Register.
Probably the saddest story it tells is of the King family who owned the
property on which the Pest House stood and who list four of their
members, two young women and two tiny children, in the smallpox epidemic
of 1784. This epidemic continued on into 1785 when twelve villagers
(see plate 15) died and there were small outbreaks in 1786, 1789 and 1790,
and one isolated case in 1805. A very crude vaccine was in use from the
middle of the eighteenth century, but the largeness of the cut needed
and the unpleasant swelling of the arm for weeks afterwards deterred many.
There are no records of vaccinations actually in Wroughton, but at least one
man from this village was vaccinated at Malmesbury during this century.
"Fever" crops up with great regularity during the summer months each
year. What kind of fever is not specified - it may well have been of
several different varieties. The average number of deaths was three
or four per summer, but in 1796 twentysix people died and several more
were unable to work full time again because of "weakness".

BURIALS.

Date.	Name of the Deceased.	Names of the Father and Mother.	Aged.	Supposed Cause of Death.	Where buried.
1785					
Jan. 29	James Dick				
Feb. 10	Frank Ward P *		that	Consumption	P.G.
ɓ 13	Tho. Buckland		68	Dropsy	N.
Mar. 10	John Matthews P		70	Dropsy ʃe	N.
13	Mary Gingel		60	Consumption	S.
15	John Richard		inf	Fever	S.
30	Mary Aston		75	Fever	S.W.
Apr. 3	Elizabeth Buckley P		63	Dropsy	S.E.
21	Robert Yeate		112	Asthma from ʃt	S.E.
May 13	Richard Farmer P		50	Consumption	S.
			NA	Small Pox	S.

* The Mark of P. is annexed to Paupers, exempted by Act of Parliament from the Tax on Burials. —

15. Excerpt from the Parish Burial Register for 1785. Details of the cause of death were only recorded between 1785 and 1812.

Consumption claimed two or three victims each year and Dropsy had about the same record. Infant deaths averaged nine or ten a year and in some families very few survived infancy. The King family and the Wayt-Kings seem to have suffered more than most in this respect. Often new babies were given the same christian name as a brother or sister who died in infancy. This was to perpetuate family names that were handed down from generation to generation.

Small items in the Church Wardens' Accounts give us a little more idea of life in the eighteenth century. For example, the men in the village had a chance of earning a few extra pence by killing vermin. During the years 1769-70 two shillings was paid for four young foxes, one and elevenpence for 1½ dozen sparrows and sixpence for a polecat. In 1771 the weather was very bad and the Church Wardens paid out for an umbrella for the Vicar so that he could "bury the Corpses" without getting wet. In 1769-70 the old school over the stable was repaired by the carpenter and the school bellows mended so at least the children were allowed a fire in school in the winter.

The Overseers did at times lend money unofficially to people in genuine distress, but these loans were their own responsibility and they could be fined if they were not repaid. Annually the Parish Books and Records had to be displayed in a public place then taken for auditing to an appointed rendezvous in the County. Altogether the work of the Overseers seems to have been arduous and the responsibility at times overwhelming, especially as heavy fines or goal sentences were threatened on official Poor Law documents for small mistakes or indiscretions.

Nineteenth Century

If administering the Poor Law had been difficult in the seventeenth and eighteenth centuries, at the turn of the nineteenth century it became well nigh impossible. A quote from William Morris, Swindon's most noted historian of Victorian times, says this of 1800 "The condition of our poor however in the neighbourhood was terrible in the extreme at this time. The dearness of food during this and the following year put it practically outside the reach of the poor to whom it appears to have been doled out as charity in quantities just sufficient to sustain life".

Bread chits were issued and most poor families (probably at this time fifty per cent of the population) lived on little else. Loaves were measured in dry gallons and baked as large as possible to preserve freshness. Families were issued chits for one to five gallon loaves according to numbers. In many parts of the country violent Corn Riots occurred where the poor thought the rich were hoarding food, but in the North Wilts area it remained fairly peaceful suggesting that the local officials did their best to cope. The main cause of the poverty was the heavy taxation on the essentials of life caused by the desperation of the Government to raise money to defend the country against the threat of Napoleonic invasion. The taxes included bread, tea, coffee, sugar, windows (many were blocked in to avoid taxation), glass and soap. Even the burial of paupers was taxed. Added to which more men were required for the army and some returned never able to work again, all dependent on the Parish for support.

Causes of Death recorded between 1785 - 1812

Cause	1785	1786	1787	1788	1789	1790	1791	1792	1793	1794	1795	1796	1797	1798	1799	1800	1801	1802	1803	1804	1805	1806	1807	1808	1809	1810	1811	1812
Excess drink																												
Unspecified	1			1												1	1		1	1	1		1		1	1	2	2
Infancy	9	9	5	4	5	10	12	2	5	6	6	5	3	1	10	2	3	4	6	5	7	3	2	7	5	1	2	2
Old Age	5	1	1	1	4	5	2	4	1	6	6	2	2	2	6	7		1	4	5		1	2	6	5	1	4	5
Accident		1	1				1		1	1		2					1	2	1		2	1		1		2		1
Suicide									1	1													1					
Execution										2																		
Fever	8	26	4	3	1	4	1	5	2		1	1					2	1	4	4	1	1	1	2		1		1
Measles		2																							2			
Whooping Cough		1				1																			3			
Smallpox	12	2		1	4	4															1	2						
Inflammation					1											1							1	1				
Putrid Fever				1																				1				
Consumption	2	1	2	2	2	1	2	7	3	3	1	2					2								2			
King's Evil												1										1						1
Venereal																	1		1						1			
Cancer												1												1	2			1
Disorder of the head																									1			
Fits			1																		1		1	1	1			1
Weakness																2												
Palsy	1															2								1		1		
Apoplexy							1											1										
Asthma																		1									1	
Dropsy	4		2				4	2	2	2		1	2	2		2	2	2	4		4	2		1	1	1	1	1
Sudden				1	1	1						1						1	1					2	1			
Childbirth						2	1	2											1					1				
Decline					2											3		4	4	4	3	3	1	5	2	5	7	4
Rupture																												
Surfeit						1																						

A great number of letters written to and received from other parishes by the Wroughton Overseers of the poor still exist in the Records Office at Trowbridge and the following selection give us quite an insight into the life of the village poor in the first forty years of the nineteenth century. These letters were sent by the Carrier carts which ran regular services to and from every parish in the country using mainly the new turnpike roads but in the more remote areas rutted tracks. Letters were usually sent to the local inn. For example the money sent for the maintenance of widow Fowler when one of her children fell ill in 1804 was sent to The Black Horse, Hampton, Middlesex.

Wroughton was responsible for all its poor people who were forced to move to other parishes temporarily in search of work unless they decided to stay and took out a certificate of settlement. In 1815 Martha Stephens who had moved to Kingston in the hope of a better life was forced to write to the overseers requesting "a trifle for clothes for Johnathan and Mary Stephens as they are quite destitute". At this time a Mr Washbourne was Overseer of the Poor. In 1815 William Jones of Princes Risborough wrote to offer him a woman to keep house and teach the poor children in lace trade. Whether the offer was accepted is unknown. These letters often contain a description of the person's character. The Overseers of St. Giles Cripplegate requested relief for Joseph Little, his wife and family of four during illness, assuring Wroughton that he was hardworking and that after recovery he would find work so that the payment would be only temporary.

If anyone was too old or ill to work in their adopted parish they were usually brought home by carrier's cart as it was less expensive to support them in Wroughton.

One rather sad series of letters concern the Miller family who in 1824 fell upon hard times in Kingsclere near Newbury. John Miller, the head of the family, got behind with his rent because trade became bad. The letter says "The times are against him having several opponents in his trade." He must have persevered because in 1831 a request for a doctor's bill of £1.2s.4d. to be paid was submitted. He was suffering from dropsy. Misfortune began to mount up as later that year his daughter died and the request for burial fees of £2 said "they have really not a shilling to help them bury the poor girl." In 1834 John Miller became dreadfully ill with dropsy and the request for help for the three remaining children stated "There is not a man in the parish who bears a better character." In 1835 Smallpox struck the family and poor John struggled to write to Wroughton himself "My wife is still very ill and I can assure you that we are in great distress as scarce anyone will come near the house, neither will anyone employ me in their own houses in consequence of our affliction so you must naturally suppose we are very destitute." Small amounts of money for the family were sent for several years.

Fathers, desperate for assistance, tried to impress the Overseers with the merits of their families. Anthony Hawkins, working in the mines in Monmouthshire, requested clothes for his sons and said, "It is the last time the boys will trouble you as their settlement will be in this county and they are industrious, tidy, hardworking lads." Unfortunately Anthony lost his hand in an accident and had to claim assistance as he was unable to work and wages in the area were very low. Maintenance was sent to "The Angel" in Monmouth.

The Overseers had the power to send people home if they considered them unsuitable for any reason. John Morgan was sent home from Taunton with his wife because "It is very singular and strange that a tailor with only one child should become a pauper unless he be a spendthrift and of bad character."

The amount of paper work was very great and letters were often mislaid or ignored so many parishes threatened to transfer large families back to Wroughton to gain quick replies. St. Helens, Lancashire, prefaced one letter in 1834 with this sentence, "We have taken out an order of removal to your township which we shall be obliged to execute unless you are pleased to spare us the expense by sending on the receipt of this town's certificate legally executed." This was for the legal settlement of a thirteen year old girl, Ann, who was pregnant but willing to settle and eventually marry the father of the child.

Not many Wroughtonians appear to have committed crimes requiring a gaol sentence but in 1833 M. Richens was in Fisherton gaol, Wyelye, and requesting £3 to secure his discharge. The parish was expected to deal with lesser offenders and in 1834 Thomas Miflin of Shaw had to complain to Mr Green about William Jacobs' non-payment of rent. Thomas says "He declares to me that he never will pay his rent. My seizing on him I am certain would be no recompense whatsoever as he has nothing of any value in the house." Mr Green on behalf of Wroughton paid his back rent then took him on as their tenant until all the arrears had been paid.

Travel allowances to take up new jobs could be applied for. The usual method of travel was on the carrier's cart but not everyone considered this suitable for young girls. A relation of Elizabeth Jerome wrote about her transport from London to Wroughton. "I greatly object to sending a young girl to be out with all sorts of company night and day. I consider it very improper and if the gentlemen do not think it worth wiles to send her by coach I hope they do not send her at all."

Throughout this period applications were made for tools to set a man up in a trade. In 1835 G. Maslen was granted a set of tools. A special cart was kept by the parish to bring bodies from other parishes home for burial.

Anyone considered dangerous to others was sent after examination by the local surgeon, to Fairford Lunatic Asylum. In June 1836 this letter was received by the Overseers:

> "Gentlemen,
>   This morning Simpkins' wife brought your order. He is certainly much better though at times very perverse which appears to arise from a bad temper. I trust he will be able to attend an employment for the benefit of his family.
>
>   Alexander Iles."

This optimism was very quickly dispelled as in October of the same year this letter arrived:

"It is hereby certified that James Simpkins of the Parish of Wroughton is now a pauper lunatic in the establishment of A. Iles Fairford is insane and requires confinement.

J. Purvis, Surgeon,"

It had never been possible for Wroughton to keep all its parishioners in full employment at home and in the 1830s a ray of hope for those unlucky enough not to find reasonably paid employment appeared. In 1836 a Colonial Emigration Agency Office in London sent posters throughout the country advertising the good life available to those willing to make a new start in Canada, the U.S.A. and Australia. Canada required farm labourers, mechanics and artificers of every description in the Montreal area. Immediate employment was guaranteed for 20,000 working class people with wages of £3 a month upwards and provisions. Some of these posters filtered through to Wroughton and by 1839 when the recruiting drive reached this area, several families had made up their minds to go. George Tarrant Maslen, his wife and eight children applied to go to South Australia. Wroughton was glad to lose large poor families as it saved much maintenance and the family were supplied with a certificate vouching for their character, health and suitability. Wroughton paid £21 for the passage of the seven older children which meant that the parents and youngest child could travel free. In this way many parishes lightened their financial burdens.

Politeness was always shown when writing to the Overseers of the poor as they were most people's last hope. Here is a letter where this is exaggerated to a ridiculous degree, written in 1845:

"Gentlemen,

With much pleasure did I receive your letter of the 28th inst. with a request accompanied with the threat of legal proceedings against me if I did not comply with your request immediately. You have nothing to do but to send my mother to me and I will with God's help, maintain her in my own house as long as God gives me health and strength to do so without compulsion. But you must bear in mind you must pay her expenses to my house and please send me word when I am to expect my mother Ann Daniel.

Gentlemen, I am respectfully yours,

John Daniels."

Wroughton, in common with most other parishes, borrowed heavily to make ends meet sums of money which they would never be able to repay. By 1845 the "Highworth and Swindon Poor Law Union" was in debt to the tune of £7,700 to the National Exchequer. Agricultural wages were rarely enough to live on and Wroughton paid supplementary benefit to many farm workers. At one time to save money, bread for the poor was experimentally baked with barley, but so much "wind" resulted that the experiment had to be abandoned.

The job of Collector of Taxes was well nigh impossible, and he usually returned with more unissued receipts than signed ones. In most cases this was ignored unless knowledge of a hidden source of revenue was available. Some parish houses were sold off to pay for essentials and the numbers housed in the Workhouse reached a peak in the 1840's.

Despite the terrible conditions there was a steady drop in infant mortality at this time, perhaps due to the appointment in 1804 of N. Washbourne as "Surgeon to Attend the Poor" at a fee of £12.12s. a year. He agreed to supply them with medicine and treat all diseases "excluding epidemic fever of the Typhus or putrid kind, Smallpox or Cowpox or difficult cases of midwifery, fractures, and dislocations, and extraordinary or capital cases in surgery". At this time the disease of Consumption became known as "Decline" which was a more socially acceptable word.

As the first part of the century drew to a close and Queen Victoria's reign began, material conditions improved. The railways were branching rapidly throughout the country and the transport of the necessities in life was easier. Once the fear of starvation receded, people began to look at their way of life more carefully and considered how it could be improved. Wroughton's main problem, together with all other parishes, was that of bad sanitation and polluted water supply. Most of the better houses had adequate toilet facilities but the poorer properties often had only smelly holes in leanto's backing up to the cottages, and any drainage tended to be into gutters or ditches on the roadside which were invariably blocked and fly-ridden. In 1851 the public health inspectors were invited to visit the village and submit a report and recommendations on improvements needed. Most of the defective properties mentioned appear to be poor or tythe cottages, as in many cases the landlord rather than the occupier is required to carry out the improvements. Here are some of the entries.

(1) Offensive accumulation of manure belonging to John Heath.

(2) Offensive drain out of repair in Field and Williams property belonging to John Hinton Price of Swindon.

(3) Offensive privy and pigswash on the premises of John Gibbs.

(4) Three foul and offensive privies belonging to Ann Smith (recommend rebuilding at top of garden and houses to be limewashed).

(5) Three offensive pigsties of Thomas Palmer to be removed from the bakery.

(6) Offensive pigwash and stagnant water to be removed from the property of Charles Prowse, harness maker.

(7) Two offensive privies to be removed to the top of the garden at "the Coopers Arms" (now "The Ely")

(8) Dead well (polluted well) snd stagnant water on the property of Mr Toomer

(9) Offensive ditch by the highway at Welcomb belonging to John Butler, farmer.

(10) Pond of stagnant water to be filled up and a proper drain to be made in front of the cottages opposite in Wharf Road on the property of Mr John Duck, farmer.

Altogether over thirty offensive privies were reported in Wroughton and one poor man, Thomas Norris, is reported as having no privy at all. One was hastily built by his embarrassed landlord, Thomas Bendrey.

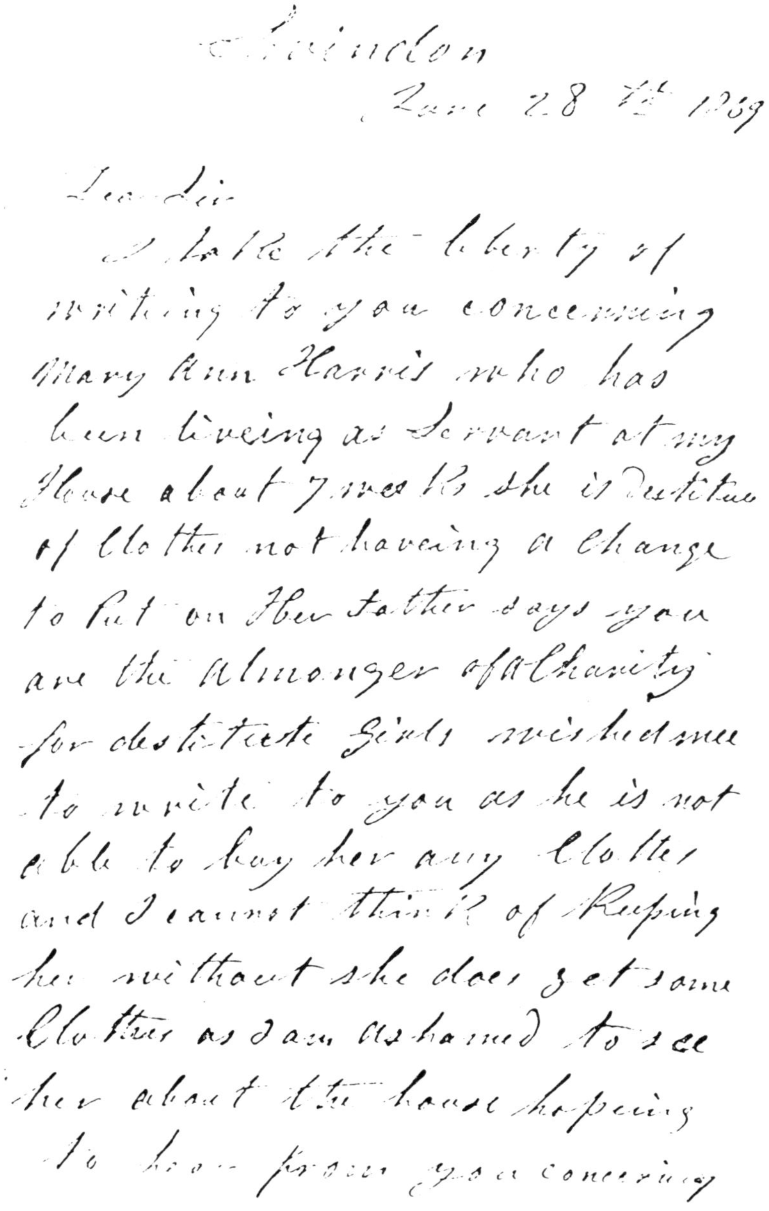

Swindon
June 28th 1859

Dear Sir

I take the liberty of writing to you concerning Mary Ann Harris who has been liveing as Servant at my House about 7 weeks she is destitue of Clothes not haveing a Change to put on Her father says you are the Almonger of a Charity for destitute Girls wished me to write to you as he is not able to buy her any Clothes and I cannot think of Keeping her without she does get some Clothes as I am Ashamed to see her about the house hoping to hear from you concering

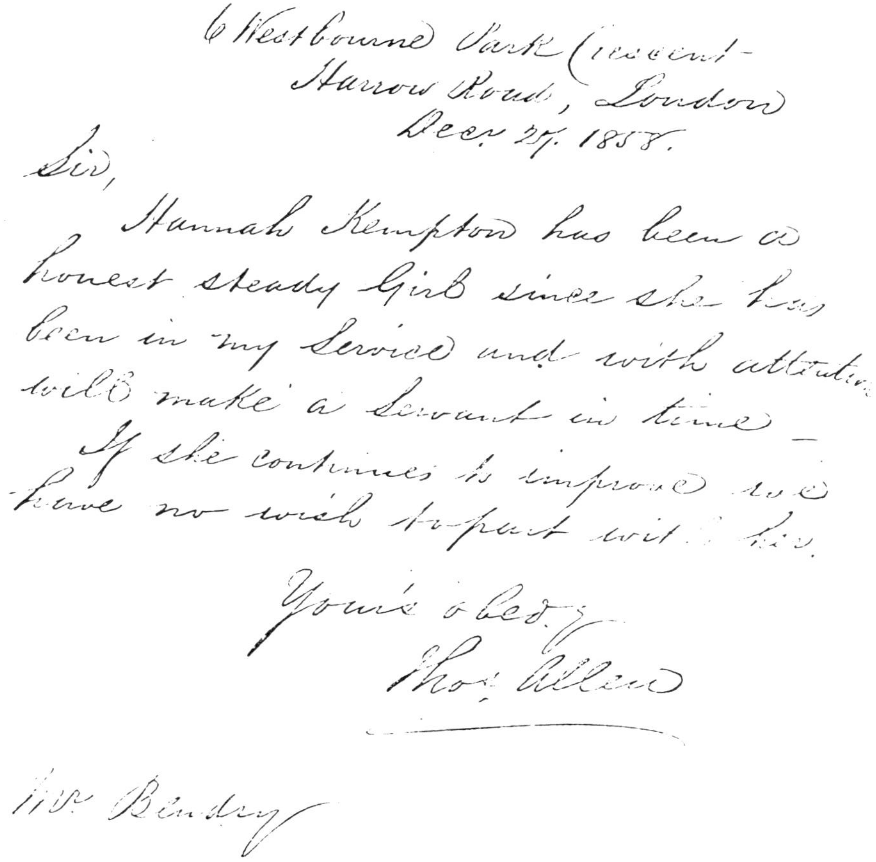

6 Westbourne Park Crescent-
Harrow Road, London
Decr 27. 1858.

Sir,

Hannah Kempton has been a honest steady Girl since she has been in my Service and with attention will make a Servant in time —

If she continues to improve we have no wish to part with her.

Your's obedy
Thos Allen

Mr Bendry

16a
16b Letters requesting the clothes allowance of 10 shillings

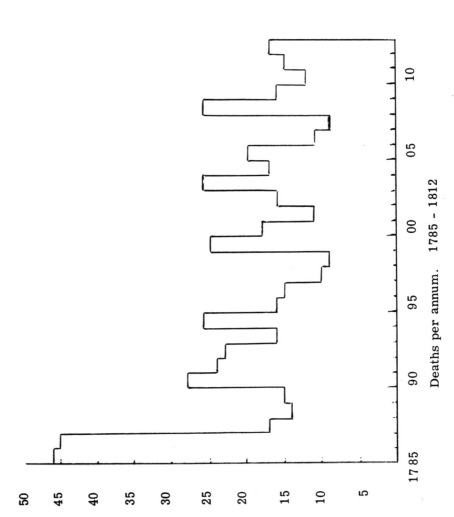

Deaths per annum. 1785 - 1812

17. Numbers of deaths depended on epidemics: 1785 Smallpox and Fever   18. These advertisements appeared in "The Church Monthly" May 1918.
1786-26 Fever deaths

Considerable improvements were made and the village must have become a much pleasanter place to live in. Outbreaks of cholera and low fever almost disappeared, especially after the reservoir was built in 1866.

The only surviving list of property owned by the Churchwardens in Victorian times was made in 1838. Out of 100 properties in the village 15 belonged to the Church Wardens with rateable values varying between £2.8s and 10/-. The Swindon poor also owned two buildings on land belonging to them on the site of the present Ellendune Shopping Centre.

By 1850 Parish meetings were held monthly in the church on Sundays. Occasional public meetings were also held there as this was the only building in the village large enough. Usually six parish officers were elected. In 1849 the following were officers:-
Charles Spackman, John Canning, Thomas Bedford, Edward Watts, John Washbourn, Jonathan Hall. Half were changed annually.

In the 1851 minutes there is a list of twelve villagers who were elected to serve as constables. This was an annual appointment but most served for several years. These were:-

William Austin	–	Carpenter
James Bedford	–	Dealer
John Butler	–	Farmer (Elcombe)
John Duck	–	Farmer (Wharf Road)
John Hawkins	–	Grocer
Phillip Pavy	–	Miller
Charles Prowse	–	Collar maker
B. Pickett	–	Farmer
Robert Prowse	–	Victualler
Charles Spackman	–	Farmer
John Washbourn	–	Farmer (Overtown)
Edward Watts	–	Farmer

In March 1851 the Pest House was in need of repair and money was allocated for this purpose.

In 1856 the fire engine was repaired and put into full working order. Mr Prowse undertook to provide a suitable house (garage) and to supervise the oiling and cleaning for £3 a year. By law the fire engine had to be tried on three days a year to make sure it was in working order. Horses had of course always to be quickly available.

Hiring fairs for farm workers and girls in service had shifted to Wootton Bassett on Michaelmas and Lady Day. Most girls found employment in Wroughton itself or the rapidly expanding Swindon. A few were dotted about in villages within a 15 mile radius and only six went further afield, according to available records four of these to London.

After the arrival of the Public Health Act in 1848 a system of stand pipes slowly spread throughout the village linked with the new reservoir on Overtown Hill. Slowly polluted wells were filled, in summer fever epidemics lessened, new houses had indoor water supplies and owners of older properties could collect water from public pumps if they could not afford to have indoor plumbing installed.

This of course did not happen in a day and the system grew slowly over 50 years as the money became available.

Very little information is forthcoming from parish minutes until 1894 when a new Local Government Act came into force. The new parish council began in a confident and enthusiastic manner but were soon slowed down by the apathetic attitude of the Rural District Council who rarely bothered to answer their letters.

By 1895 local unemployed labour was being used to dig local stone and repair the roads of the village. This was a continual struggle as lower parts of the village were often flooded and roads had to be remade. Early school log books often record low attendances at the infant school at the bottom of Prior's Hill due to floods.

A long battle with the R.D.C. began over the administration of the water supply. Replies were rare. Valves were inserted by each standpipe in case of accident so that not all consumers would lose their water. The ringing of a bell signified the turning off of water supply in an emergency. One of these standpipes stood, until recently, on the corner by the Co-op. A deep gutter on Wroughton Hill and the High Street was discussed as being a danger to children going to school. A drinking water tank was placed at the spring in Prior's Hill to provide water for the area from a pump at "The Swan". Continued wrangling went on over clearing out ditches to stop flooding, e.g. a letter asking Mr Farmer that a ditch in King's Meadow should be cleaned out so as not to block the flood water from Wharf Road.

By 1895 fifty one allotments were in use, giving people a chance of a more varied diet and more land was requested. Most people leased for one year. Many letters asking for permission to lay pipes across various people's property passed to and fro as pipes were laid to more outlying parts of the village. The Mill stream was a continual worry and repeated attempts to clear it did little to abate the flooding.

In 1896 Mr Farmer was in trouble again in Wharf Road because of an obstruction in front of the dipping places known as "The Pitt". Another bad place for flooding was "the drock" at the bottom of Workhouse Road now the junction between Wharf Road and Markham Road. The Sodom area near the old people's home in Wharf Road was very unhealthy with a polluted well and ditches with continual flooding during any wet spell. Efforts to improve the situation went on well into the 20th century until most houses had access to the main water supply.

Children had to be pretty tough to endure the winter conditions in the infant school. The log books suggest that the open fires were continually smoking badly into the rooms and temperatures were often in the thirties on cold days. Continued roof leaks left the school very damp and some days the school had to be closed to allow the rooms to dry out. The coming of education ensured that every child was seen regularly by a nurse or doctor and cases of real poverty could be checked upon. Scalp diseases and nits were the most common complaints at the beginning of the century but ointment and Cyllin soap was provided and later checks made. Epidemics of measles and whooping cough closed the school in 1917.

Having spent several years investigating the living conditions and health of the village of Wroughton in the past, I am truly grateful to have warmth, shelter, adequate feeding and health facilities such as the village provides today.

References and sources of information

Wilts County Record Office, Trowbridge
Parish registers
Letters to and from Poor Law Commissioners
Minutes of Parish Council Meetings
Charity Documents
Public Health Report 185
Swindon Fifty Years ago by William Morris.

WROUGHTON'S BUILDINGS

A first look at their origins, and their interest to us now.

by

Elaine Entwistle

There are no buildings in the parish which can at present be proved to be older than 400 years old (Overtown House Elizabethan staircase) other than the Church, whose Norman features are described elsewhere, but there are a few examples of large dwellings which have origins known to be in 17th century. In the ordinary houses of the Parish the early signs are much harder to discover, as most have been covered over, disguised or improved over the years. However, I later describe how certain features can be examined to give the approximate age of many old properties.

First it is interesting to learn how the local geology and agriculture originally affected the local building styles, and then how local industry and national fashions directed the later styles.

This area, being between the chalklands of Salisbury Plain, and the limestone of the Cotswolds, has an attractive mixture of rough and squared chalkblock, with squared limestone for the walls and even tiles of the 'better' houses. Occasionally Swindon stone is also used, as at Pavey's Mill. Another interesting feature to note in the building of the old small cottages is the use made of "Sarsens". These are large, hard, knobbly sandstone boulders which have been used as foundation stone and "in-fill" for outer and occasionally inner walls, up to around 1 metre high in some cases. It has been discovered that the sarsen stone 'sweats' and the moisture is taken up by the chalk blocks, which enables them to retain their hardness. (Large examples of this stone can be seen by the war memorial and by The Iron Horse).

Thatch has been the favourite roofing for all but the 'best' buildings since the earliest times here, due to the easy and abundant supply from the chalk arable areas. It is ironical that what used to be the poor man's roof, is now only owned by the rich, thanks to thatching costs and insurance. It is known that there have been brick works in or near Wroughton since the 18th century, on the clay lands, and it can be seen that even the stone cottages have brick chimney stacks and fireplaces. This was done because bricks are far more heat resistant, and generally more hard-wearing.

For this reason there has been much use of brick for repairing and altering window surrounds and wall corners, and even the whole front of one or two stone cottages, (e.g. in the High Street near the Post Office).

Some houses and old garden walls display brick work patterns which were used in the 17th century, but the buildings are unlikely to be that old, judging by other factors. (e.g. walls opposite the "Swan Inn" and a little higher up Prior's Hill).

Brick was used during the 18th century for many small houses and Farmhouses in the area, and some still show their attractive pattern and colour. A walk along the High Street will show you a farmhouse and Post Office house with these old bricks.

Most of the red brick buildings in the village date from late Georgian and Victorian times, and from about 1900 onwards various bricks and stucco styles are very common. Their only interest to an amateur historian is an indication of the direction, and speed, of the development of the village.

Amongst the ordinary dwellings of the Parish evidence of a very old property is hard to discover, either because it has been altered and covered over so many times, or more probably because most cottage housing built before the end of the 1600's just has not survived. (Refer to Hoskins' "Local History in England"). Very few deeds were written for small cottages until relatively recent times, and the style of these houses changed little over several centuries, until the beginning of the 18th century in country places. However, with searching it has been possible to find many examples of the various sizes and styles of habitations covering over 300 years.

Here is a brief description of the larger properties in the Parish. This gives some idea of the variation of styles, the features which are of most interest, and in some cases how little we know of our village heritage!

While there is no longer a large old Elizabethan Manor house in the village there are a number of imposing properties a little further out, - other Manor houses, country houses and farmhouses, - and there are many unique residences within the village which I include in this list, all in chronological order as far as I know it:-

1. The oldest is probably Overtown House, which contains a late 16th century staircase in fine condition, but which is mainly in 17th century style - steep roofs with attic windows, renaissance decoration, long sash windows. The west face is exceptionally attractive with its symmetrical appearance, and dates from 1672. (see Plates 19 and 20).

2. Ivery House. The original Vicarage is said to have Elizabethan origins, although a date of 1727 over the front door is more appropriate to the features now in evidence. However, there are indications that the original building may still exist within the Georgian and Victorian stylish extensions.

3. Overtown Manor (or 'Whites') consists of a long stone building with cotswold style roof, and it has a date-stone of 1693. There has been a squarer, gabled Victorian addition to the South, replacing an older part of the manor.

4. Mention must be made of the one fine old brick farmhouse still to be found within the village. This is 97 High Street where an old thatched barn is most noticeable at first. Although possibly built after 1700, (the "Femish Bond" pattern of the brickwork dates the front wall) it is a typical low linear farmhouse, originally thatched, and displaying the low front door, large squat chimneys, and low broad windows with three sections, which are all very local features.

5. Fairwater House is a unique building, constructed I would judge around 1700 A.D. in the 'new' square style, but with the older system of roofing, i.e. two single span roofs with one chimney stack between, at one end. To increase the modern look, the roof has been built above the north facade to give the impression that the roof is square, but when viewed from the Moat Walk, the south side shows the true shape.

19. Overtown House, East end

20. Overtown House, West face built in 1672

The stable block appears to be of a similar age and adds to the property's attractiveness, in spite of recent modernisation. (see Chapter 10).

6.   Quite obviously the White Hart is an excellent example of the chalk and thatch cottage which has been built in Wroughton ever since houses became permanent structures. The original fireplace has recently been opened up, and its unusually large size suggests the house may have been an Inn from the first, although the deeds and history have apparently been lost since Wadworths took charge. More will be said of stone and thatch later.

7.   Elcombe House is a fine half hipped or mansard roofed country house, built in 1740 in typical local style, with a much older wing to the west, in local brick and chalk block.

8.   Salthrop House was built in 1760, the style being much more like many country houses in the Bath area (probably from a pattern book of the time). Its main facade faces East towards Elcombe, although the driveway circles by the West. There are considerable Victorian additions (1880) on the Northern end.

9.   Wroughton House was rebuilt in 1760 and is a complex but attractive building outside, with its rows of long sash windows, and Cotswold stone tiled roofs. It contains an old staircase, said to be Jacobean. Pre 1740 artifacts have been found under a floor, and a well found inside the present house walls indicates an older smaller property. (see plate 1).

10.   Woodham House (Baker's Road) consists of two buildings, one of which is obviously Georgian (the East), while the Western end is lower and could either be an older cottage or a later annexe to the house.

11.   Chilton Farmhouse is a good example of an old chalk building which was modernised by adding an outer skin of brick to produce an attractive Georgian facade facing towards Elcombe. (see plate 21). This brings me to the old outlying farmhouses so far not mentioned:

12.13.   Southleaze, Costow, Elcombe, and Chilton Farms were bought by the Government after the First World War and split into small-holdings for ex-servicemen. They are now in the control of Wilts. County Council, and some are still in the hands of original tenant's families. All four have been split into two or three 'houselets', very badly modernised and very poorly maintained by the Council. This is particularly sad because all of them have pleasant Georgian wings and two have signs of a much earlier chalk stone building within them. Southleaze has a north facing section with a stone tiled roof, and Chilton Farm has even more stone, beams and old fireplaces to indicate its age.

14.   Westleaze Farmhouse also has a Georgian appearance, though like Elcombe House it has a mansard roof with dormer windows. It is different in having a brick front, with rough stone sides and rear. It was apparently built as late as 1800.

15.   Wharf Farm was also built about 1800 next to the new canal and is very similar in style, though much smaller and narrower, with store-rooms built at the Eastern end.

Returning to buildings within the village, the two mills are interesting:

16. 17. Pavey's Mill (Baker's Road) and King's Mill (Perry's Lane) were both rebuilt in 1771, the latter in the local brick. This mill is taller with a large date plaque and there is adjoining an older millers' house in different brick, and a hidden date stone of 1685. Pavey's Mill has a lot of chalk and limestone included in the walls inside, and Swindon stone outside; it still has its old overshot water wheel, and tall brick chimney dating from its conversion to steam in 1842.

18. Elcombe Hall is a late Georgian square plain building in fine grounds with a pleasant Victorian gate house. (see plate 22).

19. Warleigh House is similar in style - almost square, two storeys of quite long sash windows, and a shallow roof, but the eastern end is of thick stone with attractive eighteenth century rooms, while the western rooms are probably Victorian brick. Not long ago there were extensive brick stables on the northern side, and certain house windows have double sashes, apparently to enable inner gauze windows to keep out flies on hot days with horses near!

20. A small but pleasant example of a late Georgian house can be seen in the Pitchens next to the Convent. It is beautifully symmetrical, with a shallow roof but no parapet. The deeds clearly show it was built just after 1830. From the side a Victorian brick addition can be seen.

21. Three of the Public Houses in the village are obviously Victorian - The Brown Jack, Swan Inn, and Carter's Rest, all show the typical gables, decorative brick work, and very high ceilings.

22. The Three Tuns is probably an older building but with Victorian and later additions, and the Black Horse may also have earlier origins than the Victorian features suggest.

23. The only large residence built just after 1900 is The Orchards, on Perry's Lane corner, built in 1911.

Typical local features can be seen in many of the tiny old cottages which can be found, mostly in the south east of the village, but also in Overtown and Elcombe. At one time there were similar homes all along High Street and Church Hill on the south side, but many serious fires have destroyed those in the village centre, and many along Church Hill have lost their thatch.

There is no proved oldest cottage in the Parish but there are several which could eventually be discovered as such. Without the aid of deeds, documents or estate maps (as yet), there are certain national facts which may help, and other local facts which may be clues: cottage building was very similar from the beginning of the 16th century to the end of the 17th century, and the great Age of Cottage Rebuilding was from 1550 - 1660 after which there was a building recession until 1725 nationwide. (This makes our date-stones rather surprising).

There were 260 persons listed in Wroughton by 1676, and the earliest date-stones known to me, apart from the mill, are 1693 (Overtown Manor), 1696 in stone over an Overtown cottage door (Parsloe's) and 1699 in a brick chimney stack on a Green's Lane cottage. Both the latter buildings are of the single storey type, with individual upper storey windows peeping from under thick thatch.

21. Chilton Farmhouse. A chalk farmhouse with brick additions

22. Wroughton Hall. A nineteenth century residence replacing a much older estate.

They are shallow in depth (known as single span) but with very thick walls and a large wide chimney stack. The original or early stairs have gone, and Parsloe's cottages have mostly lost the original type of casement windows. The cottage shown on the front cover is of this type, but with altered windows and an extension this end of the chimney. Another cottage which is obviously as early as these is Laburnum Cottage in Baker's Road. It used to be more than one cottage, and was at one time a baker's and butcher's house, the bulge in the outer wall indicating the site of the bread oven at the side of the fire-place. Even today this property is an excellent example of an old Wroughton Cottage, but back in 1928 when a previous owner first saw it, it displayed features which sound almost original! At the rear the soil came up to the window ledge except where a tiny back door made one duck under the oak lintel. The inner doors were of solid thick wood with huge hinges and lift-up latches. The height of the rooms was six foot or less, with many dark beams displaying chip markings. The floors were cobbled - very rough and uneven, and in the bakery end were bricks and stones similarly rough. Inner walls had a base of sarsens, up to four foot in places, then wattle and daub took over. One set of stairs were very steep, more like a ladder to the upper storey. Up there the windows were at floor level and no more than a handspan in width. Over the west end there was no upper flooring - just a view to the room below. The grounds were then an acre in extent stretching down to withy beds. The present owners are preserving its old character while trying to improve its inevitable drawbacks - sarsen foundations are hopeless at damp proofing, and chalk block chimneys soak up the rain! (see plate 25)

Many more cottages of this long low design can be found, but there are also several which have had an upper storey added at a later date, usually with brick. The Paddocks in Devizes Road can be looked at closely, and the whitewash cannot totally hide the brick below the roof line, even showing the curve of the stone round the windows which were once dormers. Note the steep pitch of this tiled roof, indicating a thatch originally. This cottage has the local style windows in three sections, the centre opening.

Other small chalk block cottages were built as two storey homes, perhaps indicating a later building date, although all of these are very small, and would not have been built all that long after 1700. The lodge in The Pitchens, Appletree cottage, and number 73 Prior's Hill are all of this type, although the last lost its thatch in a fire last year. (see plate 26).

Some cottages are deceptive in that they have a brick frontage (Berkeley Cottage and 17 High Street) or brick reinforcement round windows, doors and house corners (15 & 20 High Street). The chalk was sometimes too soft, and was not really built to last hundreds of years so repairs have been carried out in more durable brick. A lot of windows were altered in Georgian times, to increase light and to be "in the fashion". Number 15 High Street has long sash windows and shutters inside, and was originally thatched, but its two storey construction and attic details suggest the whole building was added to number 13 in the 18th century.

In some cases it is difficult to know whether a property was built with a brick front and stone round the back for cheapness, or reinforced with a new, stylish brick face. Sometimes measuring the thickness of these walls can produce the answer - the walls will be much thicker with a stone lining, than with a double brick wall. Probably the properties at 18 and 19 The Pitchens are 19th century with cheaper stone rear walls, while up Prior's Hill 'The Last Chance' was probably an old thatched stone cottage before it acquired a brick face by the road.

25. Laburnum Cottage, Baker's Road in the 1940's

26. Number 73 Priors Hill. This recently lost its thatch in a fire and is now tiled.

23. Fireplace at The Lodge, Pitchens. There is a small oven with a metal door to the left of the fire.

24. Fireplace in the cottage on the front cover. There is a thick carved oak beam across the fireplace

Old photographs show this building with a thatch. Fortunately some still retain the original large open fireplaces with a thick oak beam across the opening, often carved a little to accentuate the slight curve. (see plates 23 and 24). Many of these have a small low bread oven on one side, or recesses made to hold the salt in times past, e.g. most in Baker's Road and Green's lane. Some are bricklined perhaps added as the chalk eroded. Almost all bring complaints that they smoke badly unless raised from the original hearth. Other local features of these cottages are the low beams across rooms, and very roughly shaped branches which have been used to provide the framework for the thatch. Most owners speak of 'branches', 'sticks' or 'bits of tree' in their lofts, and at least two have made a feature of these in upper rooms.

Another point raised by many owners is that at some point in its past, the cottage was two, or even three dwellings, which made them very tiny, with back-to-back chimney-breasts. Laburnum Cottage and the one opposite are good examples, and may well turn out to be workers' cottages on the Manor estate.

Humble homes built a little later than the chalk cottages are hard to discover, the only clues being a gradual change to long sash windows (as explained above) and a heightening of ceilings, and occasionally a cellar. Brickwork and a symmetrical appearance from the front becomes desirable. There are two datestones, 1787 and 1768 on houses in Green's Lane, and they show some of these features, and number 3 The Pitchens has a similar appearance, at one time being 'Waldron's Mill'.

The Post Office house was most probably built at about this time, or as late as 1800. Compare its symmetrical front and dormer attic windows with King's Mill and Westleaze, and notice the different, but still Georgian front door. As this brick building has stone side and rear walls which are all quite thick, it is possible that there was a building there earlier. The thatched cottage next door would have acquired its new sash windows and brick face when its neighbour was constructed.

Numbers 54 and 56 Prior's Hill are pretty and unusual, still showing all the features they were built with - 'Rat Trap bond' brick work and almost square casement windows with almost no recess and pleasant small panes. Bricks were only used on edge for buildings of little height - it was not so strong but more economical!

While these two are Georgian, the cottages and houses around them are Victorian and Edwardian; with high ceilings, long sash windows with large panes, and a wide shaped lintel above. The best examples of Victorian houses are Moormead Farmhouse and the houses along that side of the road as far as Jubilee Villas (opposite Pebley Beach Garage). They show the decorative tiles, ridge tiles and facia boards around gables which are so typical. A rather different example is the terrace half way up Markham Road called Pavey Cottages. Different again is the house labelled "Rectory 1889" over the door, at the top of Church Hill.

At the bottom of this hill are two distinctive late Victorian Villas, and the Towers were built in the 1880's and must be unique!

Properties lining Swindon Road, Wharf Road, Church Hill and High Street, and also parts of Marlborough Road and Prior's Hill show the expansion of Wroughton to 1900. In 1886 there were very few houses in North Wroughton - just farms and the Black Horse and one villa.

The houses showing brick work with all spacers have almost certainly been built after 1900, most with red local bricks. In 1900 there were 522 houses. Then in the 1920's the first council houses were built in and behind Perry's Lane. In the thirties more houses in Perry's Lane and those in Moormead Road were constructed. No houses were built during the war, but the 1950's saw the other council estates go up, then the sixties saw the development of the Manor and Coventry Farm estates.

This has only been a brief indication of our local building styles, an introduction to an enormous subject. We know very little about the majority of our buildings but are beginning to rectify this situation by becoming a member of the Wiltshire Buildings Record, an organisation which is recording old and worthwhile properties. Then there will no longer be the situation that a building demolished is a building lost for ever. Better still would be a depth of feeling for our Parish heritage, so that as little as possible of what remains will vanish in future years.

References and Sources of Information

The English House through seven centuries   Olive Cook.   Nelson

The English Farmhouse and Cottage   W.M. Barley

Illustrated handbook of Vernacular Architecture   R.W. Brunskill

Discovering Local History   David Iredale

How old is your house?   P. Cunnington

Local History in England   W.G. Hoskins

ROAD NAMES

by

Mary Loudwill

Some roads are so named for obvious reasons. High Street, for instance, indicates the locality of the main thoroughfare, and occurs in many towns and villages. Other names indicate geographical directions, hence Swindon Road leads to Swindon, Devizes Road leads to Devizes, Church Hill leads up to the Parish Church, and so on. But many names have more specific local associations, whether personal, historical or occupational, and they give us an insight into various aspects of the life and development of the village over many generations.

Roads with names of similar association are generally to be found within the same area of the village - like those named after aeroplanes, and those with Scottish names - but for the sake of easy reference the roads are listed here in alphabetical order. The significance of some names is uncertain or not known, but further research is being made in order to rectify these omissions.

Anthony Road	Mr Ivor Anthony was a racehorse trainer at the Barcelona Stables, which was on the site now occupied by the Convent in the Pitchens.
Artis Avenue	The land was formerly part of Artis Farm.
Ashen Copse Road	A copse runs alongside this road.
Bailey's Way	Mr Frank Bailey farmed Berkeley Farm.
Baker's Road	Formerly known as Baker's Lane. The nearby mill then owned by Mr Pavy, was leased to Mr Baker from 1858 to 1870. Mr Baker was also the tenant of the mill sited near Coventry Farm from 1861 to 1870. Laburnum Cottage in Baker's Road was once a Baker's and Butcher's shop. The grill above the window on the right is the original grill of the butcher's shop, while the bulge in the wall indicates the site of the baker's oven.
Barcelona Crescent	This is named after the racing stables (see Anthony Road).
Barrett Way	Major F.W. Barrett, racehorse trainer and owner of racing stables, lived at Wroughton Hall, which stood on the site now occupied by the Ellendune shopping centre. Major Barrett trained horses for three kings - George V, Edward VIII and George VI.
Beaufort Road	The Beaufort fighter aeroplane gives this road its name. It is one of several roads built in the 1960s named after fighter or bomber aeroplanes. Wroughton's associations with the R.A.F. are thus commemorated.
Beranburgh Field	The Battle of Beranburgh was fought near this site in 556 A.D., when the Britons were defeated by the Saxons.
Berkeley Road	The land belonged to Berkeley Farm, whose owners came from Berkeley in Gloucestershire.

Bladen Close	This housing development marks the year of Sir Winston Churchill's death, 1965, and is named after the village in Oxfordshire where this great statesman is buried.
Blenheim Road	The Blenheim bomber aeroplane gives this road its name. (see Beaufort Road)
Boness Road	This Scottish name is one of several proposed by a Scottish gentleman during his term of office as Chairman of Wroughton Parish Council.
Brimble Hill	Bremel is Old English for Bramble, and seems a likely origin for 'brimble'.
Charterhouse Road	Much of the farmland around Wroughton belongs to the Charterhouse Estate.
Church Hill	This leads up to the Parish Church.
Clyde Cottages	
Cook's Lane	This grassy footpath between Maskeleyne Way and Summerhouse Road led to the mill belonging to William Cook.
Coombe Close	Coombe or comb is Old English, meaning valley, or land in a narrow valley.
Coronation Road	This commemorates the coronation of Queen Elizabeth in 1953.
Coventry Close	The land belonged to Coventry Farm.
Cowleaze Crescent	Cowleaze Farm is nearby. Cu leah is OE, meaning cow pasture.
Devizes Road	This is part of the main road from Swindon to Devizes.
Dunbar Road	(see Boness Road).
Edgar Row Close	Edgar T. Row was a member of the Parish Council for many years. As member of the Ellendune Trust he undertook a great deal of responsibility for maintaining the fabric of the old Ellendune Hall and for the plans of the new Community Centre, which he officially opened on March 16th, 1974.
Elcombe Avenue	The manor of Elcombe is part of Wroughton Parish.
Ellingdon Road	The manor of Elyndon, or Ellendune is part of Wroughton Parish.
Falkirk Road	(see Boness Road)

Green's Lane	Formerly known as Swan Lane. Green's Mill, so named after the mill owner, was sited in this lane. The mill was destroyed by fire and the site is now occupied by Brook Cottages.
Hackpen	'Haca' is OE for hook, and 'Pen' is OE for hill. Hook hill is descriptive, the hill being hook shaped. Another such hill exists in East Devon.
Halifax Close	This is named after the Halifax bomber aeroplane. (see Beaufort Road)
Hall Close	The land belonged to Wroughton Hall, which stood on the nearby site now occupied by Ellendune shopping centre.
Hay Lane	'Hay' is OE for enclosure. This lane lies along the boundary between Wroughton and Lydiard Tregoze parishes. It is an ancient way, probably existing before the Roman occupation, and follows a straight course as part of the road from Cricklade to the Ridgeway. Six hundred years ago the road was known as the Ancient Way, also Saltharpesweye.
Hick's Close	The land belonged to Coventry Farm which was farmed by Mr Stephen Hicks, and later his son Mr Mervyn Hicks.
High Street	This is the main thoroughfare.
Inverary Road	(See Boness Road)
Kellsboro Avenue	Kellsboro Jack, trained at Barcelona Stables, was the racehorse that won the Grand National in 1933.
Kennet Road	The source of the River Kennet lies on the Marlborough Downs just south of Wroughton.
Kerr's Way	Mr Robert Kerr was Clerk to the Parish Council for many years, and owned a grocery shop in the High Street at the corner of Wharf Road.
Lancaster Road	This is named after the Lancaster bomber aeroplane. (see Beaufort Road).
Langton Park	This is part of the R.A.F. housing close to Wroughton airfield, and is named after Sir Henry Langton of Overtown House, who was awarded the D.S.O. and D.F.C. when serving in the R.A.F. during World War II.
Manor Close	The site was formerly occupied by the Manor House.
Markham Road	Also known as Workhouse Road where the Workhouse was sited. Nearc-harm is OE meaning land on a boundary.
Marlborough Road	This road leads from Wroughton to Marlborough.

Maskeleyne Way	This is named after the Maskelyne family, though the spelling is different. The family owned Basset Down House, now demolished, bought by Edward Maskelyne (1727-1775) and occupied by him from 1763-1771. He held a commission in the army of the East India Company, and his sister Margaret Maskelyne, married his friend Robert Clive of India. Nevil Maskelyne (1732-1811) became Astronomer Royal in 1765. His nautical almonacs, published annually from 1767 until his death, enabled mariners to find their longitude by observing the moon's distance from the sun. A mountain on the moon bears his name. After his death his daughter lived at Basset Down. She married Anthony Story who altered his name to Story-Maskelyne. While effecting improvements to the hillside near the house in 1822, he unearthed what proved to be an extensive Saxon interment. Two Saxon warriors were found buried, lying side by side with their shields and their spears, and with their beads of amber, glass and crystal, and knives and fibulae of copper. Not far away further interments of the same period were found. It is not known whether they fell in battle or whether this was their settlement. Their round shields of wood, with patterned bosses of iron, their ornaments and implements are now in Devizes Museum. Nevil Story Maskelyne (1823-1911) He and his friend Henry Fox Talbot were pioneers in the science of photography. In 1857 Nevil Story Maskelyne was the first appointed keeper of the minerals at the British Museum. In 1879, when his father died, he came to live at Basset Down. He became magistrate, M.P. for Cricklade, and a member of the first Wiltshire County Council. He did much useful work in connection with modern methods of agriculture and dairying.
Maunsell Way	This is on the site of the Maunsell field. The meaning of Maunsell is obscure, but is probably derived from OE 'moene' and OE 'sell'. 'Moene' means common and 'sell' is found in names of swine pastures.
Mill Close	This is on the site of the mill known as King's Mill or Seymour Mill.
Moat Walk	The moat of the Manor House was nearby.
Moore Close	Mrs Maud Moore, a member of the Cowdrey family, local builders, lived in North Wroughton. For many years she was a school manager. She was held in high regard by the local residents and has been described as 'unofficial midwife, nurse, undertaker and friend to all'.
Moormead Road	This lies on the edge of moor and meadow land.
Overtown Hill	This hill leads up to Overtown, one of the manors of the Wroughton parish.

Pavy Cottages	The Pavy family were millers and maltsters. Pavy Mill is also known as Woodham mill.
Perry's Lane	This is also known as the Bodge.
The Pitchens	Pitch is a Wessex dialect word meaning to make a path with small uneven stones called Pitchin, placed on edge.
Plummer Close	Duck's Farm was on this site. Kelly's Directory for 1915 indicates that Mr Plummer then farmed there.
Prior's Hill	The Manor at the foot of this hill was owned by the Prior of St. Swithins, Winchester.
Roberts Close	Mr Roberts, who lived in this vicinity was Vicar's warden, school manager and associated with the work of Benet's Charity and Victoria Hospital, Swindon.
St. Andrews Close	The Church at North Wroughton was dedicated to St. Andrew. It was closed in November 1967 after 32 years.
St. John's Road	Wroughton Parish Church is dedicated to St. John the Baptist and St. Helen.
Savill Crescent	Mr Montague Savill was a trainer at the racing stables at the Paddocks.
Snapp's Close	Snap is OE, meaning a piece of grazing land.
Stirling Close	This is named after the Stirling bomber aeroplane. (see Beaufort Road).
Summerhouse Road	The land belonged to Summerhouse Farm.
Swindon Road	This is on the main road from Devizes leading to Swindon.
Thorney Park	
Victoria Cross Road	This commemorates the V.C. awarded to Mr William Gosling for his gallant action at the Battle of Vimy Ridge in 1917. He was attached to the 51st Highland Division, 3rd Wessex Brigade, Royal Field Artillery. The citation for the award reads, "The award has been made to 645112 Sgt. William Gosling R.F.A., who on 5th April 1917, when in charge of a heavy trench mortar, owing to a faulty cartridge, a bomb after discharge fell ten yards from the mortar. Sgt. Gosling sprang out, lifted the nose of the bomb, which had sunk into the ground, unscrewed the fuse, and threw it on the ground where it immediately exploded. This very gallant and prompt action undoubtedly saved the lives of the whole detachment". Mr Gosling, who later served as Captain in the Home Guard, was awarded the Coronation medal in 1937. He was a dairy farmer and producer/retailer of milk at Summerhouse Farm, and died in 1945.

Weirside Avenue   This runs alongside the weir that provided power for
                   the mill known as King's Mill or Seymour Mill (see
                   also Mill Close)

Whalley Crescent   Whalley is OE, meaning a hollow.

Wharf Road   Also known as Sodom, a name commonly used for the
                   poorer area of a town or village. This road leads
                   to the Canal Wharf. Wheat was taken to Wroughton
                   Wharf to be shipped by barge to Bristol, and coal
                   was unloaded at Hay Lane Wharf after its journey
                   down the canal for sale in Swindon.

Woodland View   This cul-de-sac was formerly part of Swindon Road,
                   North Wroughton. When the M4 motorway and the new
                   fly-over road were built the part of the road which
                   was by-passed was re-named Woodland View.

References & Sources of information

Dictionary of English Field Names, by John Field.

Dictionary of English Place Names, by Eilert Ekwall.

Bassett Down, An Old Country House, by Mary Arnold Forster.

Kelly's Directory.

Local knowledge of Wroughton residents.

AGRICULTURE

by

Elaine Entwistle

Beginnings

When men began farming this area in Prehistoric times, they were just as limited as farmers still are today by the structure of the soils and the underlying rocks. As the introduction explains, Wroughton Parish has chalk and clays, divided almost across the middle by a thin band of greensand on the slopes.

It was to the chalk downlands that the first settlers who farmed came, along the ancient trackways such as the Ridgeway, so it is possible that our area had farmers as long ago as 3,600 B.C. Windmill Hill dates from then and excavations have shown that these settlers used a wooden plough, grew wheat and barley in fields which were possibly enclosed, stored and ground the grain, grazed the grasslands with oxen, long-horned cattle, sheep and goats, and raised pigs in lower forests. In these times the claylands were covered with thick vegetation and unhealthy swamp, and therefore avoided, hence the trackways.

It is not until 500 B.C. or later that there is local proof that a farming community is settled in the area, with the existence of Barbury Hill Fort. The Celts, or Iron Age people who made and altered this structure, made squarish fields which they cross ploughed with iron plough shares pulled by oxen. Signs of these fields can be seen just off the S.E. corner of the Parish boundary, on slopes facing N.E. near Barbury. They grew hulled barley and an autumn sown wheat, rye, oats and club wheat, storing them in pits or granaries. They kept sheep for wool and meat, and probably realised their importance in connection with cereal production, the manure being necessary on the thin soils.

Objects found during excavations at Barbury were all made of iron, with one coated in bronze. They suggest an agrarian tradition over many years - for example there were sickles and an anvil and hammerhead. Dates of between 200-50 B.C. have been suggested.

Incidentally, legend tells of the "Dun of Ella" being a Celtic hill fort where the church now stands. While no proof is known, and 'dun' is more a Scottish term for such an Iron Age ring fort, it may be that there was a settlement there too.

By 125 B.C. settlements were beginning on the clay lands as well, helped by the introduction of a new stronger plough. Perhaps a group of up to ten wood and thatch huts could have been seen at Ellendune, Overtown or Wertune, with the beginnings of fields around them, by the time of the birth of Christ.

This is perhaps the true beginning of farming in Wroughton. Once the clay vale began to be cleared, farming spread quickly and the parish became an area of nucleated communities raising animals and crops. This state of things can be seen clearly in the survey known as the Domesday Book.

Amongst the early charters of Wessex are brief mentions of Ellendune which indicate that by 844 A.D. there were 30 hides in production, and until 972 the estate of Ellendune is being passed on in wills. There is also brief mention of 'Wyritune' in the same will of Aelfheath which Finberg suggests is a mistake for Purton, but could possibly refer to Wertune. (see Bibliography).

27. The marks of a Celtic Field system, just East of Hackpen near Barbury.

28. A Wiltshire Horn Ram. This was the local breed until the end
of the Eighteenth Century.

So far you have read that corn, sheep and cattle have all been farmed on the chalk downlands and valley sides, and that a new plough, 'nd other developments, enabled much the same to be started on part of the claylands. Does this set the pattern for the rest of the village's farming life? Anyone who looks around the Parish nowadays can see glaring differences, and some similarities. How and when did they occur, and why? This study begins to trace Wroughton's twists and turns resulting from its agricultural development. The changes were sometimes very local, sometimes national, and occasionally the result of international affairs, and all are fascinating when related to our own ancestry and village surroundings.

The Parish at the time of the Domesday Survey

The parish area in 1086 A.D. was settled in five distinct patches, or Manors:

Ellendune (or Nether Werston)	= Church Hill area extending North and East.
Wertune	= around 3 Tuns corner, and North and East, probably.
Wervetone	= Overtown
Elecome	= Elcombe
Saltetharpe	= Salthrop

•   DOMESDAY MANORS   ☐   MEDIAEVAL SITES

The Domesday book gives quite a lot of detail:

> (In explanation of Hides and acres: in some areas, such as
> the East of England, a Hide meant 120 acres, while in
> parts of Wessex it contained no more than 40 acres. As
> we are on the edge of Wessex perhaps the latter is more
> accurate).

Ellendune having 30 hides - (at least 1,200 acres) - was the largest.
There was sufficient land for 12 ploughs and 42 workers are mentioned,
being a combination of villeins (tied to the Manor), free holders, and
slaves. There were 60 acres of meadow (which is low grassland, probably
sometimes flooded) 20 acres of woodland, and pasture of less than one
acre. Surprisingly 6 mills were within this manor, so it is possible
these early mills were partly in the upper reaches of the Ely - the
Markham Bottom valley and perhaps only reached as far as the mill we
now know as Perry's Lane Mill. But perhaps the fact that 60 acres was
low meadowland shows that the manor stretched to Westleaze mill.

The other mill was in Wertune, which is believed to be the area
around Moormead and Marlborough Road - The Pitchens, where the manor
consisted of 10 hides (approximately 400 acres). This had land for 4
ploughs and supported 15 villeins and freeholders, plus 'one Frenchman'.
Here there were only 2 acres of woodland, and 30 acres of pasture.
No meadow is listed, suggesting perhaps, no very low ground.

At Wervetone, (probably in the same area as the present Overtown
Manor and House), there were also 10 hides (400 acres or more) and land
for 4 ploughs, but there were only 11 villeins and freeholders counted,
and no details of pasture, meadow and woods. Possibly this was merely
due to bad recording, it being rather out of the way.

Elcombe is interesting: it has the largest acreage after
Ellendune - 1,080 acres or more, or 27 hides, and land for 8 ploughs.
Twenty-three villeins and freeholders and slaves worked the lands.
There were fewer ploughs and fewer people than at Ellendune. There were
60 acres of meadow, the same as Ellendune, 20 acres of woodland, also the
same, with 60 acres of pasture. The most surprising thing is that it
was valued by 1086 at £20, £2 more than Ellendune.

Saltetharpe was like Wertune and Wervetone, 10 hides (400 acres
or more) in extent, with land for 4 ploughs, and 12 freeholders and
slaves. All similar, although a lack of villeins, or 'tied' workers
must have made the running of the Manor rather different. It is just
the poorest of all the Manors at £4. Meadow covers 20 acres, Pasture
30 acres. No woodland is mentioned.

The total acreage of all these manors is impossible to know,
perhaps being just over 3,000 acres, but possibly a lot nearer our
present 6,950 acres.

A good portion of this was ploughed - thirty two ploughs were
needed for the year's work - 140 acres was meadowland, and 121 acres
were used as pasture, while 42 acres were covered with woods in
contrast to today! Overtown would also have had woodlands, and pasture,
not included above.

We can also gather that there was sufficient corn grown to
support seven mills, and that Ellendune was the main settlement,
possibly having links with the other manors through the mills.
Elcombe managed to be the most prosperous in spite of having no mill
and fewer workers. (This prosperity appears to have declined only
over the last 150 years). The omission of sheep in the details is not
so surprising when we learn that there is only one mention of them in
the whole Domesday Survey.

All the Manors would appear to have a combination of chalk and clay lands, except for Overtown, so the lack of details here is annoying. However, it seems to fit the text book descriptions of the light soils supporting fewer people, as much of the land is only suitable for rough pasture for sheep and cattle. The land when ploughed, only needs a light plough which could be manoeuvred round a rectangular field. The boundaries of these fields were sometimes mou⠀⠀⠀s of earth or stone, providing shelter for animals or crops in the worst weather. (On a map of 1885 there is clearly marked at least one rectangular field with a broad mound and hedge marked, West of Overtown Manor). Heavy soils in the clayvale, needed a heavy plough and as these were difficult to turn, the system of owning long narrow strips within larger fields began. These were known as furlongs, which were themselves part of a larger open field. The Open Field system must have been practised by some of our Manors at some time, although the evidence at the moment comes from later maps and documents as we shall see. The Manors used the chalk areas <u>and</u> the claylands. They ploughed, used other land as pasture, and the lower places were called meadows. The woodlands would have been necessary for fuel and for grazing pigs. It is debatable whether or not there was strip farming done at Wervetone, as rectangular fields were possible, but at Wertune, Ellendune, and Elecome, and probably Saltetharpe, strip farming in large open fields was practised.

So the roots of the community and the farming practices had taken hold by 1086 A.D. The fact that we still have the remnants of a Manor house in four areas (if we remember Wroughton Manor) is a welcome sign of our origins. The fifth, at Wertune, is a mystery, as it was Ellendune which was owned by the Prior of St. Swithun's, and documentary evidence shows this to be on the site of Prior's Hill Manor House, not on the hill near the church as one might have assumed.

<u>The Middle Ages</u> (Twelfth century to sixteenth century)

Large Estates and tenant farmers.

The middle Ages saw the expansion of farming with many small changes and improvements, the most obvious today being the gradual inclosure of small areas of land. Even with this, maps of the situation in the seventeenth century at least partially reflect the system used for hundreds of years. There are many glimpses of Wroughton during these times, and the national situation helps us to understand them.

The population of England doubled between 1086 and 1400 (ref. Corfield. See Bibliography) and this meant a great increase in the amount of cultivated area, inroads into woodland, and much more settlement on claylands. In the thirteenth century many manors had flocks of a thousand sheep, and wheat was the main winter corn. This must have been the case in Wroughton to support so many mills. Rotation of crops with the sheep on the fallow field meant good yields of wheat and barley. The local longhorn sheep were excellent both for their dung, while they grazed freely over many miles during the day, and for close-folding in large numbers each night. They thus consolidated the thin soils. This breed were, however, not kept primarily for their wool, as most sources explain that the Wiltshire breed had little wool, and this 'peeled' as the sheep fattened.

(More of this later). (see plate 28). No doubt the shepherds would have milked the ewes and made cheese and butter, as they are known to have done even in Victorian times.

Besides winter wheat, oats and barley were also grown, and sometimes beans and peas, - vetches, were grown in the spring. Barley was used for ale which was the main drink, not water or milk.

In the middle of the fourteenth century the Black Death resulted in the decay of over half the villages in England, and a large increase in sheep pasture to use the lands laid waste, so several deserted mediaeval village sites could date from these times. A slightly freer life for the labourers would have resulted from these times, due to the scarcity of labour.

There are many references to Wroughton Parish Manors in the Middle Ages, including Ellendune, Werston/warston and Wer'weston; Costow; Salthrop and Elcombe but only occasionally is the farming detail included.

In 1210 Ellendune was the fourth most valuable amongst the Priory of St. Swithun's Wiltshire Estates, and included stock such as 22 oxen, 100 sheep and 16 pigs. Slightly later it is explained that there are nine tenants (including four millers each holding ½ hide) and most of their arable land is divided between two fields. Seventeen virgaters used marsh for the rest of the year, their own lands had to be used for the flocks for the rest of the year. By 1387 the Demesne (Lord's farm) was leased. In 1541 it was the second most highly valued estate in Wiltshire belonging to the Dean and Chapter of Winchester.

Because Ellendune manor extended over the whole length of the parish it contained a good balance of soils. Sheep-and-corn husbandry in the south and pasture farming on the clay north.

The Rectory estate was a separate entity, and in 1249 the rector admitted ploughing one of his meadows and so depriving a tenant of his pasture rights. In 1341 it included arable land, with some meadow and pasture. In 1210 Tewkesbury Abbey's estate at Overwroughton had farm stock of 16 oxen, 27 ewes, 20 hoggets, and 15 lambs. A hayward, carter and dairyman were among the servants. (Would the last have milked the sheep?) It is thought that horses took over the ploughing on the lighter chalk soils by about 1500, but oxen would have continued to plough and pull carts on the clay lands for longer. Field names even in the nineteenth century reflect this past use of oxen. In Wroughton there was "ox-leaze" and "ox-pen" in the Northwest corner.

Elcombe is described in a volume of "Wiltshire Inquisitions" as being in 1287:

"1 messuage. 140 acres of arable land, 16 acres of meadow, and pasture in common for 50 oxen"

There was pasture in Blagrove plus one windmill. Rents in the form of hens, pigs and eggs show that farms had these too. (A messuage was one farm and its outbuildings). By 1361 there is the same acreage but only seven acres of meadow (a gradual decrease since 1086) with common pasture for "4 working cattle, 12 oxen, and 200 sheep".

Elcombe manor farm acreage varied a lot until the fifteenth century when Elcombe became the centre of an estate which included Salthrop Manor and other lands outside the parish. J.H. Bettey says that much of the claylands had already been enclosed into small family farms before 1500 or was enclosed by piecemeal agreements between tenants during the 16th and 17th centuries.

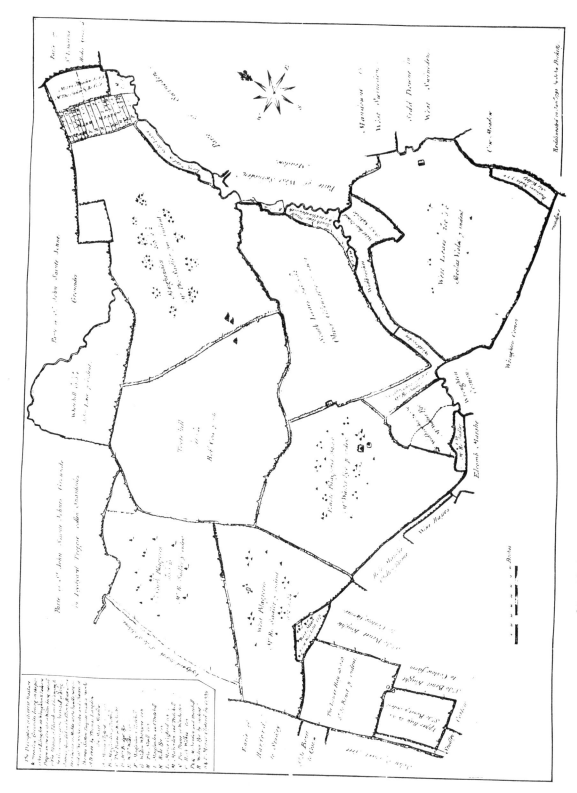

29. 1616 Map of the North of the Parish (Copy made in 1795)

30. Chilton Farm, looking Northwards over the claylands, from the
Chalk hillside.

31. Southleaze Farm, on a slight rise in the flat clay land

There are at least four sites in the Parish where once there were mediaeval villages. One, at Overtown, is a recognised D.M.V. site just to the south of Overtown House, in the area most probably settled by 1086. The bumps and dips indicate where buildings and roads once were (known as "croft and toft"). Another, on one side of Salthrop house, also shows the "croft and toft" feature well, and could have origins in the 1086 settlement of Salteharpe.

Quite near this, on the Quidhampton side of the Bassett Down road, is another D.M.V. site, which may or may not be just inside the parish boundary. The last site known to us has an interesting location in the North of the parish. There is a large clear area of "croft and toft" undulations just to the south side of Mill Lane between West Leaze Farmhouse and stream bridges to the East. An adjacent field shows long undulations which could be the ridge and furrow markings of mediaeval ploughed fields. The site is very close to the site of Waytes (or lower) mill, and V.C.H. research suggests that there was a settlement called Westcott before West Leaze, which had links with Westlecott above it.

There are still many documents to be examined to discover more about the early agrarian history. Wroughton Manor records exist for 1275-1861, but as they are stored in London, Winchester and Trowbridge, and are written in Latin or difficult script, research will take some time.

From early in the seventeenth century there is more documented evidence, and the first maps to provide a more thorough picture of the Parish agriculture, as documents never explain locations satisfactorily. However, to provide a reminder of our very particular situation at the edge of the chalk, and to provide a clue as to the way our farming is naturally progressing, we can do no better than quote J.H. Bettey:

> "In Wiltshire the chalk and the clay, or cheese country, are
> perhaps more clearly divided from one another than anywhere
> else in the Wessex region, and the distinction has given
> rise to the saying 'as different as chalk from cheese'."

Agriculture throughout the Stuart's Reign. (1600-1750 approx.)

The earliest maps of the parish are of the Charterhouse Estates, which included Elcombe and Salthrop but excluded all of Wroughton itself. These were made in 1616 and are beautifully drawn and coloured, and well worth examining if you visit the County Records Office. They show that by this time much of the Elcombe area was still under the Open Field system with much division into long thin strips (see Plate No 30) and rectangular plots around habitations. There are large fields to the East of Elcombe Street, named "Robert Sadler", and titles indicating common pasturage, e.g. Over Mead.

Further west at Chilton and Salthrop the fields are a mixture of wide and narrow strips belonging to Salthrop, Costow and Studley estates, with a band of large fields round Chilton Farm, and another area round Salthrop Farm belonging to these large estates entirely.

To the North the farms of Blagrove, Southleaze and Westleaze are all completely enclosed and separately farmed (see plate No 29)

The V.C.H. Vol. XI states that by 1633 A.D. there were about fourteen farms on the Elcombe estate. Chilton Farm had all its arable land consolidated on the downland, while on the clay Blagrove had been divided into North, West and East Farms, but the pasture of these was bad because of its wetness.

32. 1616 Map of Elcombe. Detail of Elcombe Street

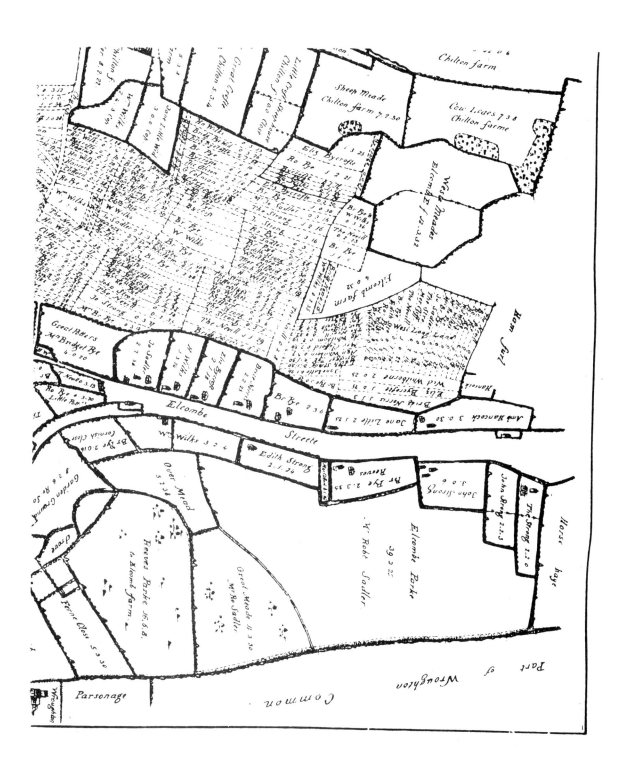

South and Westleaze were excellent pasture farms. A deed
dated 1660 between the Charterhouse and Sutton and J. Sadler of
Chilton shows the 'Messuage or Manor House' to be a fine place with
dovehouses, orchards, etc., meadows, commons, pastures and 'feedings'
totalling 116 acres. With the lease is also given:

> "The Royalty of Hawking, hunting, ffishing and ffowling within
> the premisses"!

Our only glimpses of Wroughton itself in 1616 are from the labels
around the Charterhouse maps: 'Wroughton common' where Common Farm is
now, and to the West of our Wharf Road, and 'Wroughton fields' south of
Markham Bottom. An inquisition on one 'Robert Kemme, Lunatic' of Elcombe,
lists his estate in 1638 as having 6 oxen, 7 cows, 4 young horse,
2 calves, 2 mares, 140 sheep, 4 pigs. There was also wheat, barley,
peas, beans and 'fatches' (vetches). This does show the use of oxen and
horses, and illustrates well the combination of cereals with sheep,
together with animal rearing.

In 1649 the Ellendune demesne farm had four pieces of enclosed
pasture, 78 acres in the Lammas meadow, 300 acres of arable in common
fields. Later evidence shows one field to have been high on the downs
at Hackpen and another was called West Field, on Market Hill. (?)
There were 20 acres of 'sheep down' for the demesne flock, 70 acres
of grazing for cattle and 30 acres for horses.

The Rectory land early in the seventeenth century consisted
chiefly of arable lying scattered in the Upper and Hackpen fields of
Wroughton Tithing. It also included marsh in East Field, a few
dispersed acres of meadow and 4 acres of inclosed pasture. Later there
was a little more inclosed pasture. Later in this century the arable
was divided between Lower Field, where a $\frac{1}{4}$ was left fallow, and Upper
Field, of which a $\frac{1}{2}$ was left fallow, it being poorer land. The
document describing these lands in 1671 also mentions that certain
rents were according to the price of corn, and that the buildings
included a cowhouse, carthouse and stable, so there must have been some
animals.

Many of our present thatched cottages and larger houses were built
before 1700, so we can assume that Wroughton was in fact a thriving
community by this time.

Larger farmhouses and 'Manor houses' with parts built by this
time include Overtown House and Manor, and Parsloe's cottages; Elcombe
House; Southleaze; Upper Salthrop Farm, Wroughton House and Ivery House,
Wroughton Manor and Fairwater House, and of course all the stone
farmhouses which have now made way for the housing estates, such as
Duck's and Coventry Farm.

John Aubrey, Wiltshire Historian, has written much about North
Wiltshire farming in the 17th century. He says that farming was still
a rather unspecialised occupation. The cattle were a mixed lot —
commonly black, brown or deep red, mainly pied. It was a common practice
to bring black cattle from Wales for fattening, before sending them on
to market in London.

He also explains a system of renting herds of cows to a
dairyman; the cows were rented for the year, the dairyman paid rent
for each cow, and in return was given pasture, fodder, a house and
dairy and made his money on the milk and cheese. It was regarded as a
good way up for a young man. Perhaps this system prevailed here, with
rich farmers owning the corn areas too, and being unwilling to work
the long hours a dairy herd involved. Much milk was used for cheese,
the surplus cheeses to be sold at Marlborough Cheese Market, which
was famous in the 17th century, and continued to be so.

The next piece of documentary evidence of parish farming comes from a map of 1738 and a terrier of the same year, detailing fields and acreages of Salthrop House and Salthrop farm. The map shows a few fields North of Salthrop house (an earlier building than the present one) which were being given to the Charterhouse in exchange for Salthrop Farm. The old field names are all included. The terrior gives the acreage of pasture and meadows as 111 acres. Arable and sheep pasture covers 115 acres, intermixed with Benet's estate, and there are also 64 acres of meadow and pasture intermixed with Costow and Studley farms. This sounds very similar to the situation of well over a hundred years before - 1616.

A few signs of old drainage and irrigation methods have been found, and probably date from these times. Some bits of drainage 'pipes' have been found in the fields sloping to the Ely from Haskin's Garage area. These were constructed of chalk slabs leaving a tunnel often filled with loose stones along which excess water could run. In the fields between Swindon Road and the eastern parish boundary are the remnants of an irrigation system known as 'water meadows'. Channels cut from the stream to surrounding fields would lead water to them enabling a very early crop of grass or hay to be grown in the spring, and improved use of the meadows in dry spells.

We have an excellent example of a farmer in Elcombe in 1744, in an inventory of John Herring, now kept at Swindon Reference Library. It lists his possessions, stock and equipment, and as it also mentions the rooms in which they are to be found, we can tell he was quite a well-to-do man. Here is a brief summary of the document:

Stock: 5 hoggs, 7 store pigs, 14 milch cows, 2 fatting cows,
          5 heifers, 2 calves, 114 sheep.

Crops: Oats and Malt (in the malt house)
          an oat rick, 2 wheat ricks, a bean rick
          7 stacks and ricks of hay
          Beans, vetches; old beans and old wheat in store.
          20 hundred of cheese

Equipment: 2 waggons, 2 dung carts, 2 plows, 4 harrows,
              1 roller, harness (for what?)

This farm seems a typical one, having a large interest in milk production and cattle raising, with crops for winter feed, but also growing wheat, oats and barley and keeping sheep and pigs.

Most of the evidence for this section has come from the records of the big landowners: the Charterhouse Estates and the Dean and Chapter of Winchester's Estates, with occasional documents referring to individual farmers and their lands. This shows that while a large part of the land is still owned and directed by a powerful few, there are now a great many tenant farmers who farm some of their land in larger, enclosed chunks. This should have aided efficiency in many ways, but it was a fact of life that the well-run farm was more likely to bring a rent increase, the result being a poorly run farm or frequent change of tenant.

Some evidence, which I have included in the next section referring to Wroughton Manor Estates, does indicate that Wroughton still had a lot of open fields and common pastures, right up until the Act of Inclosure in 1795.

While there has been a vast increase in the amount of land in use, and the numbers obtaining a complete living from it, it is almost startling how similar are the methods, crops and even actual farms seven hundred years after Domesday records. Yet in a brief half century three kinds of influences suddenly and irrevocably altered our parish's whole life.

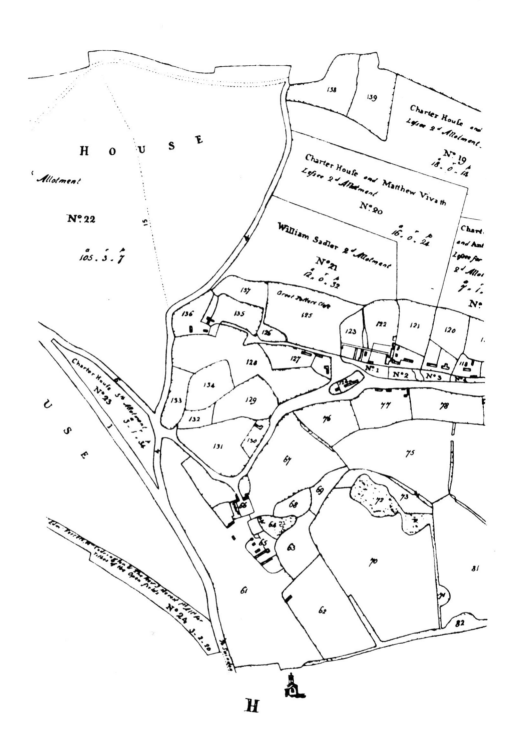

H O U S E

'Allotment

Nº 22

105.3.7

Charter House and
Lessee 2d Allotment.

Nº 19
18.0.14

Charter House and Matthew Vivath
Lessee 2d Allotment

Nº 20
16.0.24

William Sadler 2d Allotment

Nº 21
12.0.32

Chart
and Ant
Lessee for
2d Allot
7.1.

Nº

138   139

137   Great Potters Close
136   135   125
126
123   122   121   120
128
127   Nº 1   Nº 2   Nº 3
134
133   Nº 1
132   77   78
131   130   76
U S E   64   75
Charter House 5th Allotment
Nº 23
3.1.4   68   69
72   73
65   64
1   65   63
70   81
61
62   71

82

H

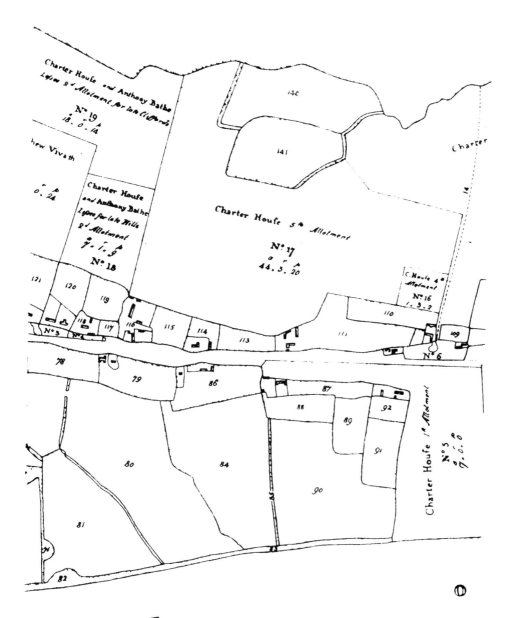

33. 1795 Inclosure map of Elcombe Street

Roads, Innovations and Inclosure (1750-1800)

The Turnpike Roads began to be constructed through this area from 1750 onwards, and for the first time it was easy to travel to other towns and regions. Although this will be examined in later studies, certain agricultural possibilities and changes must be noted now. Travel to the markets - Marlborough, Highworth and further afield was made much easier; news of new farming practices or experiments, tools and stock came faster; the whole atmosphere in England was for change and improvement. Signs of this feeling in Wroughton include the rebuilding of two mills in 1771, and Westleaze and Elcombe farmhouses built in 1800. (The coming of the canal in 1796 carried on these developments, making even faster travel possible, bringing new trading possibilities).

Any history of Georgian times will give the reader more details of the agricultural progress and change made in so many ways: the growing of such crops as turnips as animal fodder thus making the slaughter of many cattle and sheep unnecessary in the winter; new implements and machines such as seed drills, better iron ploughs and harrows, increasing yields and quality of crops tremendously. The founding of the Bath and West of England Society nearby in 1777 may have helped to introduce these. Even political events such as the Napoleonic Wars forcing the increase of home produced wheat and a great increase in its price; the inclosure of land; all these must have had a greater or lesser effect on Wroughton farmers over these years. Certainly the inclosure of the last common areas brought the most noticeable change to the land, as we shall see from contemporary maps.

A collection of documents called the 'Evans Collection' at Trowbridge gives a good idea of the estate owned by the Dean and Chapter of Winchester between 1771 and 1795 when 8 'Lots' were offered for sale. Leases were for a term of 21 years, and it appears that the Landlord was usually a professional man - a surgeon, then a Reverend Evans who let the holdings separately. One deed of 1771 to William Brown details the land very exactly as follows:

18½ acres of arable land (more or less) lying and being dispersed in the common fields of Wroughton, that is to say

3½ acres of arable in the East field of Wroughton in a place called Longstead
2 acres of arable land in East field - 1½ acres in East field - 2 acres of arable land in East field - 3 acres arable in East field - ½ acre arable in West field - ½ acre arable at Crow(?) bridge - 1½ acres in Upper Field of Wroughton in Redlands - 3 acres arable in Upper Field in Rushally Furlong - 1 acre arable in Bodge Field in Wroughton - and pasturage feeding and common for three Rother beasts and one horse leaze and quarter in the common.

Twenty five years later the Act of Inclosure ends this system of agriculture, and the whole estate is sold, split as follows:

1. Manor House, tenant John Mifflin   valued £34.10s.0d.

2. Desirable Farm 145 acres meadow and pasture
   155 acres arable, large barn, yard, commonage
   for 400 sheep, 7 cows or 8 cows alternately
   and common for 10 horses, tenant Thomas
   Washbourn   £110. 0s.0d.

3. The Valley House Woodhouse garden and
   small close let to the churchwarden of
   Wroughton   £2. 2s.0d.

4. A house built of stone, stable and
   slaughterhouse ... let to Geo. Carpenter   £3. 0s. 0d.

5. Small garden ... W. Pickett   12s. 0d.

6. Compact Farm with 50 acres meadow and pasture
   land, with dwellinghouse and outbuildings,
   orchard and commonage for 26 cows   £100. 0s. 0d.

7. Hackburn Farm containing 225 acres arable,
   dwelling house, 2 barns, stable, cowhouse,
   cart lodge and granary, orchard and garden
   containing about 5 acres and a piece of
   meadow 2½ acres called the 5 halves.
   Commonage for 200 sheep in Wroughton Field
   and 300 in Hackburn Field. Tenant ...
   Henry Gale.   £60. 0s. 0d.

8. 30 acres woodland lying on the Southside
   of Markham Bottom known by Clouts Wood ...
   average yearly produce of the underwood.   £34. 0s. 0d.

Separate Sale Particulars for number 2 state its
total acreage as 591 and a pencilled note
indicates that the tenant bought the farm (he
became a well known name in the village).

In 1794 the Dean and Chapter had agreed to inclose Rectory estate
lands for W.W. Codrington, the lands being hitherto scattered
throughout the common fields of Wroughton Tithing, and afterwards
becoming Rectory Farm.

There is more information about inclosure in maps of the time:
Comparing two maps of Elcombe (see plate No's 32 and 33) it is clear
that the newly enclosed areas have parallel or even rectangular
boundaries and are very large. In general, the smaller and more
irregular the field is, the more likely it is to be an ancient one,
not a new inclosure. New fields now owned by one farmer, were
previously worked on by 40 individuals, maybe more. Elcombe House
Farm was built at this time (see plate No.36).

It must have been similar on the Wroughton farmlands, although
we only have the post-inclosure map to work on. Following the guide
as above, and remembering that most old field hedges were kept, it
seems that most of the northern areas, once common, and the area called
'Bodge', all the eastern side (East Field?), and all the southern slopes
close to the village (upper Field?) were newly enclosed. There are a
few farmers who are obviously important in the village, but altogether
there are about thirtythree different names on the fields in 1796.

By 1802 the population had reached 1100 and the "persons
chiefly occupied in agriculture" numbered 274.

There is an extremely interesting book, for its information
about our area, written about agriculture in 1800 (published in 1811),
by Thomas Davis. It is called "A General View of the Agriculture of
Wiltshire" and can be seen in Swindon Reference Library. Bearing in
mind that it refers to North Wiltshire generally, it gives a good
idea of the local situation and changes taking place. On the subject
of inclosure he states that between 1794 and 1811 common fields
between "Broadtown, Elcombe, etc." which required draining, were
inclosed. Many would become more valuable if converted into pasture
from arable, previously being too wet for sheep in the winter. He
does explain that the mole plough is already being used to temporarily
improve wet lands for up to seven years. The state of farms and
properties by 1800 he describes as being, in part possessed by
"great proprietors, who lease it out in small estates for lives
renewable" but many especially in the North had been much divided, and
freeholders created.

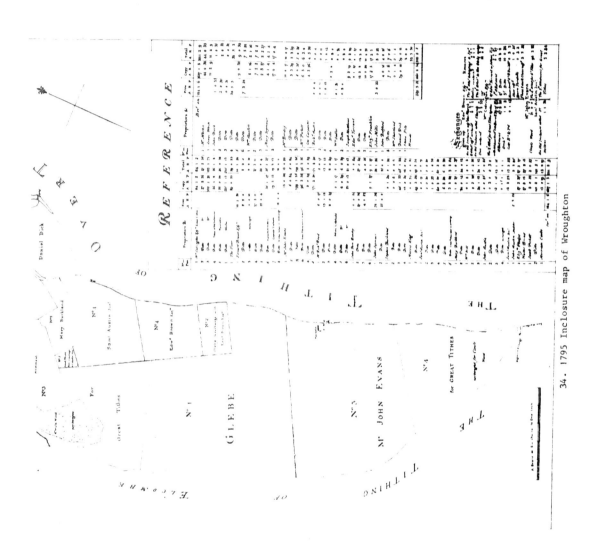

34 . 1795 Inclosure map of Wroughton

"North Wilts dairy farms are usually very well accommodated with buildings, particularly with milk-houses and cheese lofts ... The cowsheds, calf houses and milking yards are also in general on a much superior plan to those in many other counties". The dairy has in part, lost ground to grazing (dry cows, or sheep, for winter fattening, or sheep from downland farmers). A fourteen year lease was most common, although there was also the 21 year lease, which I have found locally. Animal husbandry was beginning to change, to wintering cattle in stalls, and spreading dung on mown lands later in the year. Davis states that the 18th century preference had been for the old Gloucester cow "a sort now almost extinct". The new craze was for longhorned or "North Country cows". Supposedly they gave more milk for cheese, and more meat when fatted, but he believed there was more pride than usefulness in their ownership.

Great numbers of Devonshire or Herefordshire cattle were brought in in early spring for fattening. They were fed on last year's grass or hay, or potatoes, etc., before being sold to Hampshire, Bath or Smithfield market. There were only a few oxen left by this time locally. On the subject of sheep, Davis explains that a newer type was replacing the horned native-to-Wiltshire breed. The newer breeds matured within two years, and were therefore eaten younger. Other references explain that the Wiltshires were unsuitable for breeders as they were hard to fatten, had "not wool on the belly" and both sexes had large horns. Even so there was resistance to change, as they were tough, used to travel, and were scanty feeders. It was thought that the lack of wool growth led to a greater growth of mutton. A shepherd speaking about 1840, said there was a solitary flock of pure bred Wiltshire sheep in the county then, but many shepherds had never heard of them.

Sheep fatted for sale were bought at Michaelmas fairs and wintered on land too wet for cattle. There were professional graziers for this occupation, but there were also dairymen who did this. Pigs were a necessary appendage to every dairy farm. Usually they were a mixture of long eared white with the "black african or negro pig".

Returning to Cheese making: the local cheeses were becoming as famous as Gloucester cheese, and Davis commented that even with differing soils and grasses the dairy-women were excellent at their job. More of this later. The cheeses were sold chiefly to factors who contracted for it yearly.

So as the 19th century began, our area was changing dramatically with its new lay-out and improving productions. The Parish appears to have been thriving and prosperous, with dairying, animal raising and corn production all important factors in its success. Strange then that Davis should remark:

"Wiltshire labourers are strong and robust ... but there is a remarkable slowness in the step, not only of the shepherds, whose laziness is proverbial, but also particularly of the ploughmen, and which they also teach their horses" ... "and it is not only at the plough, but in all other kinds of employ, that this indolence is visible; it seems instinctive in the whole district, even in the children".

No, not here!

19th Century Progress

The population in 1802 was 1100, the vast majority living and working within the parish. The Wilts and Berks canal was being constructed by then, and was completed in 1810. It brought some problems to the lower mills, as provision was made to draw water from the River Ray and land was used to make this possible. The route used for the canal was already marshy and was therefore not a great loss to the farmers.

Once business began on the canal, not only the quiet lives of the North West corner of the parish were altered: the recently increased yields of corn could be sent out more quickly and profitably, while lime, peat ashes and other manures could be brought in; other products such as malt and cheese were sent out, and tools and implements brought in (along with talk of the latest inventions, no doubt).

Alfred Williams tells of one trick employed by the bargees to obtain some of the wheat; they inserted thin straws into the loose loads of wheat, and dripped water down these straws. The grain swelled, and when the wheat was off loaded it was counted by weight, any surplus being left on the barges. Naturally the bargees had seen to it that there was always some surplus!

During these years the dairy side of farming was extremely important for the production of cheeses. From being a mainly local commodity it had grown through the centuries to being an important money-making concern and North Wiltshire cheeses were as well known as Gloucester and Cheddar by the nineteenth century. There are several description of cheeses and methods by this time, but briefly the situation was this: there were three types of cheeses made; thin cheese, broader thick cheese, and loaf cheese. The last was more skilled, the best quality, made from full cream milk and it included a dye to make the colour like beeswax. Thin cheeses were soft, made in early spring and sent weekly to London, or matured until autumn and sent to Reading Fair by land or water. Broad thick cheese was made later and matured for longer. There was little butter made during the cheese-making time. Every dairy had its cheese room, and pigs were always kept to make use of the whey. The canal would have aided the cheese industry locally. It was in 1830 that William Cobbett travelled from Wootton Bassett to Highworth and remarked in his "Rural Rides" that this area ... "is a cheese country, some corn, but generally speaking it is a country of dairies".

Also in the 1830s a carter (reminiscing to Alfred Williams about his work at King's Mill) was well used to seeing the courtyard piled with wheat, and knew that the mill also ground bones for use as manure.

However, the disruption the canal caused to the community was nothing when compared with the next arrival in the area. Although the railways only cut across the north west corner of the Parish, their influence was quick and permanent in Wroughton. Little need be said of the building and expansion of the Works in Swindon after 1841. Compare the number of men connected with the Railways: in 1851, according to census returns, 12 men were listed as Rail labourers, Engineers, etc., and in 1871, 90 men similarly listed. In contrast, agricultural labourers dropped in number from 346 to 125 in the same interval.

35. Costow Farmhouse. Built following inclosure of the area

36. Elcombe Farmhouse. Also built around 1800, with a dairy wing

An initial effect was to offer secure jobs with good wages – very tempting to agricultural workers. Once the railways were in full swing, all the advantages the canal had offered farmers were increased by the rail network: tools, machinery, new breeds of cattle, artificial fertilisers, drainage pipes, were all brought in more satisfactorily, while it became a cheap and fast outlet for farm produce.

The 1868 cattle plague in London cowhouses was far from a disaster to Wroughton farmers, as it necessitated the start of liquid milk sales to London by train. The Chippenham milk factory began in 1873.

But did steam lure men away from agricultural jobs or were there already too many men, after the war, or was it the use of steam in agriculture which left labourers without jobs?

We know that Pavey's Mill was converted to steam in 1841 (the chimney's still there). The mill near Coventry Farm was converted to steam in 1854 and King's Mill was equipped with a steam engine in 1860. Apparently Bedford's Mill, now under the reservoir, also had a tall chimney. This conversion may have been due to one or all of the following influences: coal now came cheaply from the Radstock area along the canal; corn could be sent out direct to new mills via the canal, so more efficient methods of grinding locally had to be found; perhaps it was a sign of increased yields of wheat, and increasing prosperity; and of course steam power was the new modern development!

In 1871 there is mention of an "Engine Driver, flour mill" and two men termed "Engine Driver threshing machine" in the Census. It is known that a steam plough was used at Overtown House – this being the efficient new way to increase the acreage of corn on the chalk, breaking up old rough pasture. These were still being used within living memory.

Richard Jefferies wrote about this area in such books as "The Gamekeeper at Home" 1878. One particularly relevant passage refers to 'local' mills. "Comparatively little wheat now is ground in rural places, the greater portion is carried away to the towns and turned into flour by steam". He adds that the buildings would be occupied by several families and their garden would be over the mill pond. In a large scale map of Wroughton in 1885-6 it is clear the Westleaze mill is indeed disused. Lower Mill (near Beaufort Road) is labelled 'corn' as is Seymour Mill (Perry's Lane). This is surprising as V.C.H. XI states that by 1865 Seymour Mill had ceased working as a mill. The stones found there then included ones for bone and seed milling. The land on which the highest mill was situated was obtained by the Water Company in 1866 to form the Reservoir.

We are ahead of ourselves again. To return to life at the start of the railway era, we have a valuable collection of source material with maps of the 1840s onwards, additional survey material, and the first detailed census of 1851.

In a book called Wiltshire Tracts, 136, in Devizes Archaeological Museum Library is an old Moore's Almanac with scribbled entries on the empty pages. These were written by C. Bradford in 1812-13 and are the daily accounts of Westleaze farm. There is much mention of buying or selling one cow, colt, etc., etc., tools, equipment and crops, but as no dairy produce is alluded to, I assume this was entered in a different notebook (although it is possible that this tenant did not do any dairying).

He certainly had many 'grazing cows', heifers, bulls and calves
and a great many oxen, - labelled Glamorgan, Devon or 'Heriford',
at times, - to my surprise as T.Davis had found no evidence of
oxen being bred in North Wilts 12 years before. There were also
many horses, mares, colts mentioned, all of which leads me to
suppose the farmer preferred to raise animals on his grassland, to
sell them to surrounding farmers, many of whom are listed. There
was also a lot of traffic in sheep: in September 75 ewes and rams;
in June 80 lambs sold; next September 47 fat ewes sold to various
places and 30 more in October. Wool and 239 fleeces were sold in
February and April. I find it surprising to find so many sheep on
the clay lands, although Davis did explain the reasons. I found
one reference to a side of bacon, so perhaps a pig or two were kept.
The writing was difficult and cramped, but malt, pease, oats and straw
must have been bought in, as they are listed with coal. I enjoyed
finding, among a list of expenses, "Mrs Cripps silk hose". Compare
this farm description with a report of 1878 later in the study.

A map and detailed survey of 1843, to accompany the Tithe
map stored at Trowbridge, gives a clear picture of the size of each
farm and type of farming carried out there. As we would expect,
all the lowland farms, Westleaze, Costow, Southleaze and Blagrove
have all pasture fields - a total of 982 acres. (The two in the
N.W. corner include Willow Beds). There are many helpful field names
like Cowleaze, Drove, Ramsmead, Horse ground and Mare and Colt
ground. All the others have a combination of pasture and arable.
Hackpen has three times as much pasture as arable (perhaps showing
rough pasture around Barbury); Overtown Manor/East Hackpen has a
mixture, with the pasture round the house, including 'Cowleaze',
and round Barbury. Overtown House has ten times as much arable as
pasture and is the next to the largest holding. The largest farm
is Upper Salthrop, which has twice as much pasture as arable.
Salthrop House itself only includes 100 acres of pasture and woods.

Chilton nearby has a third of the acreage under arable,
this being a narrow patch up as far as the Red Barn area, while
the two thirds of pasture stretches just west of Elcombe past the
canal and road line. Here such names as Bull, calf and sheep meads
occur.

The most surprising information given is the totals of
cereals at that time in Bushels and decimal parts of bushels:

Wheat	561.88328
Barley	996.60351
Oats	1434.50505

This indicates more than twice as much oats were grown as wheat,
and a lot less wheat was grown than barley, although wheat brought
the highest price.

The 1851 census contains fascinating glimpses of the Parish
at this time. Agricultural details can be gleaned from the occupa-
tions of the individuals in each family - even some of the children -
and from some farm names and short descriptions of each area
covered. If only the enumerator had walked down lanes and tracks
to each dwelling in turn, how much more informative it would have
been! Again, anyone scanning the spidery script will soon earnestly
wish that the writer had been more inquisitive, instead of being
satisfied with the vague description "Agricultural Labourer".
However, we can at least be aware that out of a population of 1645
there were 346 whose chief occupation was "Ag. Lab.", plus 29
persons who were farmers, bailiffs, etc.

There were 18 farms mentioned, though for Rectory Farm no acreage was included. Most farms also have the number of men, women and boys employed there, a few labelled as dairymaids or plough boys. Salthrop is by far the largest farm, with 1,800 acres, with 58 men, 50 women and boys. Possibly this is because by 1846 Upper Salthrop and Quidhampton were worked as one farm.

The next are Overtown (meaning the manor) with 600 acres, and Elcombe farm with 400 acres. In 1853 Overtown House had 410 acres of arable land, chiefly for wheat, also beans, peas, clover and vetches.

By 1871 both Salthrop and Elcombe have reduced acreages, Rectory Farm has 453 acres, having become part of the Codrington estate in 1869, but Westlecott and Chilton have their acreages omitted. The improved detail shows us that Westlecott, West Leaze, Southleaze, Blagrove, Costow and Elcombe all have dairyworkers as we might expect on claylands, (Chilton seems to have ceased much of its farm work for the moment), while Salthrop, Red Barn, Hackpen, two Overtown farms and Elcombe all have shepherds, (and there are two shepherds living on Prior's Hill). There are 24 ploughboys listed - all were aged between 9 and 15.

In the 1879 Journal of the Royal Agricultural Society of England is a report on a Farm Prize Competition 1878, at which West Leaze was one of 4 winners. The tenant James Beavan sometimes sold milk to Aylesbury Dairy Company, but in May was making cheese. He had 186 acres of pasture land, and 40 acres of arable. The stock included 49 dairy cows, 12 two year old steers and heifers, 23 yearlings, 4 working oxen, and a bull. 150 Hampshire Down breeding ewes and later 64 ewes and lambs. 30 small pigs had been purchased when cheese making was resumed. Three cart horses and a nag were kept. This farm still kept oxen, hundreds of years after most farmers had ceased using them. The sheep husbandry seems very similar to that 60 or so years before, but the dairy farming is what one would expect of this area, and the temporary change to cheese making indicates that there was no 'overnight' conversion to permanent liquid milk sales.

However, it was during the 1870s that national conditions began to bring changes to certain parts of farming.

Recession and war

By the 1870s there was a general recession lasting until 1914, part of the cause being unseasonal weather, bad harvests and a drop in corn prices following cheap imports. The corn laws had been repeated in 1846, and from 1870-1890 the acreage of corn shrank by 25 per cent over all the chalklands.

A fall in the price of wool hit some farmers badly, coming at a time when the bad weather brought foot rot to sheep, and there was less acreage for them. In Wiltshire, sheep numbers dropped by 1/5th, and by 1950 sheep numbers had dropped by 90 per cent. Of course the railway's transportation of artificial fertilisers was another nail in the coffin for sheep farming, sheep manure not now being necessary.

Cheese making suffered a decline not only because of the railways. True, the liquid milk business became the major concern of most dairy farmers, but cheese was still being made at times, in the seventies and eighties as we noted at West Leaze. It was the increase in hygienic methods and standardisation which eventually killed the cheese making. (V.C.H.Volume IV page 100). It was more difficult, for technical reasons to standardise or establish quality control in the case of Wiltshire cheeses, so by the First World War little remained. Berkeley Farm was built towards the end of the 19th century as a cheese making farm, with pipes direct to pig sties, so the end was obviously not foreseen. Cheap American cheese would have contributed, as would the cold wet summers, bringing a decline in grass and hay, and therefore milk.

There is a map of 1885 which shows the beginning of the loss of land through building, along the Swindon Road at North Wroughton mainly. There was also a gradual loss along the road edges on all the main roads (see Building study). From this time land was increasingly being bought for housing rather than agriculture, the price being far greater than a farmer could afford. This still holds true today, when building permission is given.

I recommend to you Alfred Williams's book "Villages of the White Horse" as it gives some specific tales of Wroughton Characters and places and much general information about our area before the First World War. The copy in Devizes Library (Wiltshire Archaeological and Natural History Society) has a letter from him to the Goddards of Swindon explaining his aim in writing the book. He hoped to portray the essence of the area with accounts and descriptions of about 1900.

It is difficult to quote bits which illustrate 'essence' but some facts of the parish should be noted here: He stayed at Upper Salthrop Farm and talked to the farmer, named Ferris. There were stacks of wheat, oats and meadow hay, and there was clover and sainfoin. Cattle and sheep were farmed on a large scale. The farmer told him that sheep farming was better because "this chalk is heavy and cold" and corn only did well in dry years.

Mr Williams travelled by the side of the 'coomb' and noted that one side was cultivated and the other was wooded (Clouts Wood).

An old shepherd he knew in the village had sometimes in his seventy years been in charge of a thousand sheep, and they sometimes gave 1,200 lambs.

Alfred Williams quotes one of his memories: "Back in '79 purty nigh every ship an thase downs died, aa, an' hers an' rabbuts, too. Tha'ed the flooks, tha's summat in the liver, 'an ther was no stoppin' on't".

Shepherds around the turn of the century are also mentioned in past village magazines. In the 1972 magazines there was regularly an article about an old shepherd, Maurice, who had worked at Overtown "long afor the Whites, must have been the Retters who owned the land then. As a boy, (seventy years before) I remember twas all sheep, as far as the eye could see up to Mudgell and Barbury. The shepherds had little cabins on wheels and used to stay night and day with the sheep". One particular cabin he describes was spotless and there was a "girt side of bacon hanging up aside the stove".

"We had about 2,000 sheep on our side of the downs, but the man who owned the land above Barbury had nearly double that number ... Course, when twas lambing time, twas even more." All the shepherds in those days wore "them cord weskits" and there was a tradition among them at Christmas time that they should dress up and visit neighbours and villagers with their accordians.

There are just a few other references to agricultural life up to the first world war: Apparently by 1906 traffic on the canal had ceased. There is one example of Estate Agents' sale particulars in these years: in 1907 the trustees of the Codrington Estate sold Hackpen Farm, including two enclosures of pasture and about 66 acres. At this sale they also advertised "The Manor House, an Elizabethan residence, moat ... gardens, etc." ... and six enclosures of "rich accomodation land" presumably near the bottom of Prior's Hill.

Agriculture locally during the war years is a subject which needs separate study, preferablv before all eye witness accounts are lost to us.

Up to the first World War the situation was, as ever, 'chalk and cheese' with many farms having acreages which covered both types of soil and therefore two main types of agriculture: arable on the good chalklands, grazing on the poorer slopes; dairy on the clay lands.

Only the details and methods were undergoing changes by this time: the sheep were fast disappearing from the downs, and the farmyard pigs from the dairy farms as cheese making ceased for good. Wroughton Parish was still a parish of farms, but with a fast extending residential area housing commuters to Swindon and beyond.

There follows a personal account of local farming from the twenties' to the present, which hopefully rounds off this study by enabling us to see both ends of our farming background from our standpoint of "the present".

References and Sources of Information

Prehistoric Britain	K.Branigan 1974
The Environment	J.D. Banes 1973 Batsford
The Domesday Book 6 (Wiltshire)	Philimore 1979
Anglo Saxon England	Peter Hunter Blair 1956
The Early Charters of Wessex	H.P.R. Finberg 1964
From Alfred to Henry III	Christopher Brooke 1961
Rural Life in Wessex	J.H. Bettey 1977
Rural Economy of Gloucester	William Marshall 1976 (reprint 1979)
A General View of Agriculture in Wiltshire	T.Davis 1811
A guide to the Industrial Archaeology of Wiltshire	M. Corfield 1978
Victoria County History Wiltshire Vol. 4	1959. XI 1980
Rural Rides	W. Cobbett 1821
A Shepherd's Life	W.H. Hudson
The Gamekeeper at Home	R. Jeffries 1878
The Villages of the White Horse	A. Williams 1913
Sheep Husbandry and Diseases	A. Fraser 1957
Wiltshire Bibliography	Goddard 1921

The copy at the Museum Library, Long St., Devizes, (Wiltshire Archaeological and Natural History Society) is an 'Open Sesame' to all the Wroughton material held there.
Wiltshire Archaeological Magazine. All volumes. See above.
Maps and documents at the County Records Office indexed under Wroughton, Elcombe and other headings.
e.g. The Evans Collection 212A/38/14/1-6 Concerning Wr. Manor Charterhouse lands etc., etc., 361/1-8 and more.
Census Returns for 1841 - 71 on microfilm.

A WROUGHTON FARMER'S MEMORIES

by

John Gosling

In fairness to those who may be brave enough to read these lines about the farming scene in Wroughton, it must be clearly understood that the writer is no great academic researcher into the serious history of agriculture, and this is merely an attempt to set down a lightweight, sometimes interesting and occasionally an amusing account of the memories of one who was born into a farming family in Wroughton during 1925.

In September of 1908, my father's family moved into Artis Farm, North Wroughton, from a similar type but smaller farm at Lower Wanborough. My grandfather had recently died from an injury sustained when he fell from a hay-stack, so my grandmother became the tenant of "Squire" Goddard of The Lawns, Swindon.

The Goddard Estate, I believe, in those days consisted of eight or nine farms around Swindon, from Shrivenham Road through Walcot to Coate and Broome Manor, and including Artis Farm and Westlecott Farm to the West of Croft Road, the latter being the only farm remaining in the ownership of the Goddard family today.

My early memories of Artis Farm, where I was born in 1925, and of the village were probably of scenes not so very different from those of 1908, although some development had taken place. The first Council house had been built at the eastern end of Perry's Lane, or Bodge, as it was known locally. Some private housing had also been provided in Moormead Road between Barretts' Wagon Works and "Bill Dykes" Garage, now known as Pebley Beach.

Looking eastwards and westwards from Artis Farm could be seen only green fields and hedgerows topped by tall elm trees. None of the land in the valley was under the plough, and the dairy cow "reigned supreme!"

There was little change to the buildings at Artis Farm until 1936. The cow stalls consisted of low, stone walled and red tiled buildings around three sides of a stone yard, with very tall elms bordering the fourth side of the square. These magnificent trees provided welcome shade for the livestock in summertime, and a useful windbreak in the winter. There was an open-sided "Dutch Barn". which stands in good condition to this day, providing cover for hay and straw, and a few wooden framed and currugated iron sheds and stables.

The milking cows were tied by neck chains during the winter months, and were allowed a short exercise period in the mornings, during "mucking out". What wonderful progress has been made over the years in cow housing, today most dairy cows, which are still housed during the winter months, have freedom of movement from strawed, covered yards or cow cubicles to water and food throughout the day and night.

Prior to the year 1918 my father produced milk at Artis Farm for the London market, and because milk in those days had a limited 'keeping' quality, it was essential to deliver it to the milk platform at Swindon GWR station by 7.30 a.m., to ensure that it was loaded on an early train to Paddington.

37. Mr J Gosling Snr. with shorthorn cow in old yard Artis Farm 1920

38. Milk float with large brass churn. Artis Farm 1923

I remember my father telling me how he would start milking by 4.30 a.m., and after being cooled the milk would flow into 17 gallon churns, which would then be loaded into carts and hauled to the railway station by horses. The reward for all this was the princely sum of 3d. per gallon! It was not surprising that at the end of the first World War my father decided to try his hand at retailing direct to the housewife in Swindon, and on his first day he sold 4½ gallons!

During this period between the two world wars, it was not unusual for dairy farmers within easy reach of a sizeable town, to retail their milk direct to the housewife. Wroughton farmers were well placed for this type of direct selling, the roads were good and the distances not too great for the horse-drawn milkfloats.

Among those involved in the retail trade were Billy Large of Toothill, Tom Ellison of Common Farm, William Gosling, my uncle, of Summerhouse Farm, where Langton House now stands, Mr Wiltshire of Berekley Farm, Mr Archer of Belmont Farm and my father, John Gosling, of Artis Farm. All these at some time had milk-rounds in Wroughton or Swindon.

Competition for customers was keen, and two deliveries per day, morning and late afternoon, were quite normal. At Artis Farm, I remember that as soon as enough milk had been cooled from the afternoon milking, a young man with shoulder yoke carrying a bucket each side, complete with measure, would set off along North Wroughton to fill the jugs of those who wanted really fresh milk for tea!

How different is the milk trade in 1982. Because of the general improvement in production methods with a subsequent improvement in hygiene quality, and the introduction of the Pasteurising process, it is now possible to keep bottled milk fresh, under refrigeration, for at least a week or even longer. This makes it possible for the future introduction of a reduced deliveryservice, and indeed this trend has already started with the six day per week delivery. There is a continual battle, within the industry, to keep costs down, and regrettably this may lead to a reduced level of service.

By 1920 milking machines were becoming popular and I understand that one of the first Alfa-Laval plants was installed at Artis Farm in 1922. This development caused the beginning of the decline in the numbers of men employed in dairy farming. Whereas in the early days of handmilking ten men would be employed to milk 100 cows, it is not unusual today for one operator in a milking parlour to milk 150 cows.

Until 1969, when monster machines started digging and levelling at the Black Horse for the M4, it was usual for the Guernsey herd at Artis Farm to travel the length of North Wroughton to reach the pastures at the northern end of the farm. Naturally the slow passage of some seventy cows caused considerable inconvenience to other road users. On one occasion during a particularly hot summer's day in the mid-thirties, the cows were leading a motorcade of cars, lorries and buses, when a fashionably dressed lady-driver expressed her impatience by continually sounding the horn. The cowman who was plodding along at her side, looked in at the open window and said with great feeling:- "Ah missus, them aal got 'arns but em caint blow em!"

In fairness to all those who regularly suffered so much inconvenience, it should be stated that over a period of about sixty years only one accident between car and cow was reported. This occurred when an anxious farmer tried to force his way through the herd. He excused his impatience by explaining that he was "late for milking!"

The field at the northern end of the farm, through which the M4 now passes, was always known as the Black Horse field and was named after the 'Pub' which bordered the main road at its western end.

The Black Horse field was, between the wars and into the fifties, well known for the sporting activities which took place over its green sward. The Swindon Education Authority rented some ten acres of its total of eighteen acres, for the provision of four or five soccer pitches during the winter months. During the late twenties and thirties, Swindon Rugby Football Club also had the use of the centre of the field, and the erection of the tall rugby goal posts each year was a sign that winter had arrived. The landlord of the Black Horse, a popular and well known character called Clarry Yeates provided the rugby players with changing room facilities and suitable liquid refreshments when required! For many years the narrow end of the field, near the 'Pub' was used by the Swindon Hockey Club.

The soil formation of the "Black Horse" unlike that of most of Artis Farm, was of a lighter and more open textured type, which drained naturally and made the field ideally suited for many other open-air events such as village fetes, pony gymkhanas, donkey-derbys and political meetings to name but a few. The "Black Horse" field also provided the people of Swindon with their first opportunities to see real aeroplanes "taking-off" and "landing". Apart from its well drained soil and level nature, the field was shaped like a long triangle, which was eminently suitable for the operation of light aircraft, of the type used during the twenties and thirties by the various air circuses which became popular during that period.

Several famous airmen brought their Aero 504's and De Haviland 9s and Moths to the Black Horse field to give five or ten shilling "flips" to persons, young and old who were eager to experience this new and exciting form of transport.

Capt W.E. Jordan, a 1914-18 fighter pilot, who during the second world war ferried American aircraft to beleaguered Britain, and later became chief pilot and general manager of Jersey Airways, was a regular visitor to Wroughton with his three-seater BLACKBURN bi-plane. It was he who gave me, in company with my sister, my first ever ride in a "string-bag" at the age of five. With his fur-lined leather jacket and silk scarf he was to me the real BIGGLES hero!

Campbell Black and, I believe, Cathcart Jones, who won the London to Sidney air race in the early thirties, and Sir Alan Cobham of Flight Refuelling fame, were also among those pioneer pilots who flew from the "Black Horse" field.

The reader may be wondering what all this has got to do with farming in Wroughton! I can only try to justify my digression by suggesting that it may be of some interest, to those who, like me, have a genuine love for and interest in flying, to know that Wroughton was a part of the aviation scene long before the military airfield was ever planned.

Early in 1943 my father purchased Berkeley Farm which adjoins Artis Farm, and was therefore a valuable addition to the farming enterprise, and was an early example of the now common practice of buying up adjoining land in order to create a more economically viable unit. Wood Farm was added for this reason when it was put on the market in 1966.

Berkeley Farm buildings are interesting, because they were erected at the end of the nineteenth century for the specialist operation of cheese-making. The dairy was connected by a glazed pipe to a large underground, brick-lined tank. This was used to store the whey, which is the bi-product of cheese manufacture, and was conveniently placed next to the pig-sties for easy feeding to the pigs. The cheese room over the dairy, where whole cheeses were stacked for "ripening", is still intact today, although it has been used for many purposes since those times. During the 1939-45 war, various village organisations used it as a meeting place, because the Ellendune Hall was requisitioned for defence purposes. I can remember the ladies of the W.I. singing "Jerusalem" overhead while down below could be heard the "clink" of milk bottles and the boom of milk churns.

Alas the traditional milk churn is no longer part of the farming scene in Wroughton. Since the seventies all milk has been stored overnight in refrigerated stainless steel tanks, and discharged into motor tankers daily for onward transport to processing and bottling dairies.

Much of this milk is taken to the St. Ivel dairy at Wootton Bassett where it is pasteurised and bottled and then supplied to local distributors in the Swindon area.

In one comparatively short life-span the milk industry has progressed from the polished brass milk churn on horse drawn float, with tinned measures for dipping milk into pint and quart jugs, to the highly sophisticated, mechanised and computerised business of the 1980's.

No mention has been made yet about those farms in the South of the Parish which consist of mainly arable acreage.

In the early thirties my father was given the opportunity to take his first steps into the "fields" of arable farming, when fifty or so acres at Prior's Hill, owned by Mrs Maria Washbourne of High Street, was offered to rent. With the help of the late Mr Cecil Witcombe, son-in-law and part time farm manager for Mrs Washbourne, and perhaps more importantly the village schoolmaster, he began to learn the business of growing oats and barley and wheat.

In the beginning at Prior's Hill, only horses were used for ploughing and cultivating and of course at harvest time they were essential for pulling the 'binder' which was a development from the 'reaper' and delivered neat and uniform sheaves, automatically tied with string, and deposited in rows, ready for the gangs of helpers who followed the 'binder' and built them into 'stooks' or 'shocks'.

When the sheaves were sufficiently dry, after a week or more, they were 'pitched' onto wagons, again pulled by horses, and taken to ricks where they would stand until threshing time during the following winter.

39. Hay wagon with Violet in harness and school party aboard 1929

40. Muck spreading with horses 1929

To haul the necessary wagons and equipment to Prior's Hill was a major problem, because of the gradient of Prior's Hill itself. Sometimes it was necessary to 'station' a trace-horse at The Swan, and the horse would be hitched up in front of a horse and wagon, thus doubling the 'horse-power' to haul the empty wagon to the top of the hill!

It was not until later that the first Fordson tractor was introduced. Tractors in those days were mounted on iron wheels with iron cleats which dug into the soil as the wheels turned. One of the problems with the early tractor was that the highway authority objected to the use of iron cleats on the roads. Large iron bands were therefore fixed around the tractor wheels, before it could be taken from one part of the farm to another. It was also considered wasteful to pay a road fund licence, so the tractor was hitched up behind a Shire horse, and towed from field to field. Much to my joy and satisfaction from the age of eight onwards, I was allowed to sit on the tractor and steer it behind the horse. It would seem that in those "civilized" days a vehicle was not considered a motor vehicle so long as its engine was not running!

The increased use of machinery of all types, and tractors in particular, brought about an increase in the number of accidents to farm workers and others on the farms of those days. In the absence of legislation controlling the use of machines, it was a matter of relying on the common sense of individuals. The "Health and Safety at Work" Act was of course unheard of and many serious accidents occurred.

An example of this type of accident happened in the summer of 1931, during haymaking in a field off North Wroughton. I was riding with my father on a Fordson tractor, which was hauling an iron-tyred "boat" wagon, which in turn was hitched to a mechanical hay-loader (rather like a mobile elevator), and with two men on the load we were collecting hay from the swathe. During a sharp turn at the corner of the field, a front wheel of the wagon sank into soft ground, and the load which was almost complete rolled over on to the rear of the tractor. My father stopped and with great difficulty eased me from under the hay to safety. The two loaders had also managed to slide down as the load toppled. It was not realised until a few minutes later that a local boy, named Albert Card, who had been walking alongside was now trapped under the hay. His cries for help could be heard and at that moment smoke was seen rising from the hay which covered the rear end of the tractor. I was quickly despatched to tell Mr Decketts, who was the sub-Postmaster in North Wroughton, to call the fire brigade. My father and the two loaders set to work to release Albert from the furiously burning hay. This they did at the very last moment, when the heat was becoming too intense. Luckily Albert escaped with no more than a strained back and bruised ribs.

Most of the equipment was totally destroyed, but the heroine of the night was a mare called Violet. At the height of the fire it was decided to hitch Violet to the front end of the tractor in order to pull it clear, because there was a very real danger of the fuel tank exploding. Violet was backed towards the tractor and after securing the trace harness, she was "given her head" and she pulled the burning tractor away, where the flames could be dealt with by the firemen from Swindon.

This episode, which so nearly had fatal results, was a salutary lesson for all concerned, including my father!

I seem to have digressed from my description of the arable enterprise at Prior's Hill! Our main crops were wheat, barley and oats. The wheat was sold to local merchants who, on Monday market days, sat at their desks in the Corn market which still stands within the walls of Swindon Cattle market, but is now used as a timber store. Samples of grain would be carried in small cloth bags and presented to the buyers for their inspection, and usually after a period of good-natured banter a deal would be struck and a price agreed.

Only the surplus barley and oats was sold in this way, the remainder being used as food for the dairy cows at Artis farm. Some root crops, mangels and swedes were also grown to provide food for the livestock.

A small area, about one acre in the corner formed by 'Coombe Bottom' and the Barbury road was permanently set aside for the growing of Lucerne, which was in great demand for the feeding of racehorses at the various training stables in Wroughton. I was not aware of any business arrangement with the trainers, who seemed to help themselves as required! Perhaps it was considered a privilege to provide fodder for such famous race-horses as Brown Jack and others, or maybe the occasional 'tip' was given in payment!

During the early part of 1939, changes took place to the South and West of Prior's Hill. Firstly, a large tract of land including Rectory Farm, owned and farmed by Mr Ernest Manners, and other land to the east, was purchased by the Air Ministry. We learned that an airfield and a military hospital were to be built.

Rectory Farm was approached by the narrow lane which leads off the A361 at Red Barn, and although on the higher chalkland was a mainly grassland farm. Ernest Manners was among the vanguard of farmers who applied liberal dressings of phosphates to chalk grassland with outstanding results, and who was quick to appreciate the possibilities of "ley farming". Old and worn out permanent grassland was ploughed and after taking a crop or two of cereals, was seeded with the newly developed strains of highly productive grasses.

He described his farming practices in a successful book published in 1953 called "Land is what we make it". From this book I learned that Rectory Farm was to have been leased by the War Department during the 1914-18 war, and an Officer of the Royal Engineers had already arrived to start the necessary clearance for a military Reception Station, when in 1917 the project was halted. It was perhaps as a result of this earlier interest in the site that the Air Ministry finally purchased the whole in 1939.

The war years saw great changes in the Parish. Apart from the loss of land for the airfield and hospital, a factory for the production of gun-turrets was erected in North Wroughton, on land formerly part of Berkeley Farm, and further land at Brimble Hill was used for several years by troops who practised the art of digging slit trenches! The whole area became a maze of zig-zag white strips which needed much careful treatment after the war to restore it to its former fertility.

After the war and during the fifties saw the loss of further parts of Berkeley Farm, with the development of Berkeley Road and Artis Avenue. This was closely following by the sale of Coventry Farm and the Manor Farm in Wharf Road, and eventually Mr B.V. Berry's pig farm fell victim to the developers as they pushed further northwards.

Because the boundary of the former Borough of Swindon had already been moved many years previously, the M4 did not in fact pass through the Parish of Wroughton in the area of Croft Road, although several farms further to the west were adversely affected.

It should not be forgotten that where the motorway passes through low-lying wet areas such as we have in the north of the Parish, the advantages of improved drainage for the surrounding land are very real. Long sections of the River Ray and the Swymburne from Croft Road back to Hodson Wood were cleared of weed, deepened and widened. These main water courses had last received this kind of beneficial treatment at the end of the second world war, when much of the manual work was undertaken by German prisoners.

Over a period of fifty or sixty years, the type of produce from Wroughton farms has changed but little. The lower lying farms still mainly concentrate on milk production, although a few now have land under the plough and practice a form of mixed farming producing milk and grain. The farms above Wroughton village are mainly arable but often also support a milking herd or a beef enterprise.

The techniques of farming have changed greatly. Productivity has increased because of advances and improvements in the breeding of animals and plants, and the development and use of sophisticated machines and computers.

The young farmer of today, often college trained, is well equipped to take advantage of the technological revolution which has taken place, and with his knowledge of modern livestock and crop husbandry and the means to monitor, to measure and record performance by group use of computers, he is well placed to compete successfully in this modern and very competitive world.

Sometimes the very fact that great economic pressures are exerted, results in a clash of interests between those who wish to use the land for their enjoyment, and the farmer who needs to make a living. This competition for land use is naturally more acute around the larger towns and villages, and many farmers in Wroughton Parish are often "in trouble" with the local inhabitants. Sometimes a footpath has been obstructed or mud from agricultural vehicles has been deposited on the roads, or the smell of silage is unpleasant and, the most serious nuisance of all, the smoke and ash from burning straw has drifted over the village.

It is to their credit that the people of Wroughton are generally very understanding and forgiving, but the farmer must not take this for granted and should make every effort to minimise the nuisance.

Wroughton farmers have played an important part in the general programme of tree planting, which became so necessary after the decimation of the elm population by "Dutch Elm" disease during the seventies. Much of this effort will not become apparent for many years, but with luck and the passage of time perhaps the Wroughton landscape will once again be blessed by the stately elm, as it was in 1925, where my story began.

WROUGHTON AIRFIELD

by

John Gibbs

In 1937 a large expansion of the R.A.F. was planned, and aircraft were becoming more sophisticated, so the Air Ministry prepared for a corresponding increase in the Maintenance Group. Thus No.15 Maintenance Unit was established and the site chosen around "Rectory Farm House". As well as the farm, there were gallops on which horses from the local stables were trained, and there was a small disused chalk quarry.

During 1939 work started on levelling the site and digging foundations for the hangars and buildings. The main purpose of the Unit was to receive aircraft from the factories and prepare them for active service.

A temporary grass landing field, one mile from the chosen site, was used until spring 1941. Heavy rain could make the grass landing area unserviceable and made it very difficult moving aircraft to the various hangars and dispersal areas. The stored aircraft had to be dispersed, with some up to three miles from the airfield, and movement was hampered by a lack of tractors. By summer 1940 lessons that had been learnt from early aerial combat showed modifications which had to be incorporated in new aircraft. Fitting self-sealing fuel tanks called for round the clock activity and at night planes had to be moved across fields by torchlight. This was very tedious when moving them for testing their guns at the butts constructed under the shadow of Barbury Castle.

A decoy town target was maintained by a small group of men on top of Barbury Castle.

The first concrete runway, 4750 ft. long and subsequently increased to 4890 ft., was aligned to give the longest possible path extending from the South-West corner to the North-East edge. Because of its exposed position on the edge of the Downs, winds could easily stop the use of this runway and another was built crossing the first on an East-West axis of 3750 ft. The third runway was completed on 13th March 1944 and is 3999 ft. long. All three are standard 150 ft. wide.

Towards the end of 1941 the establishment reached its peak with over 700 civilians.

Up to early 1943 the work was predominantly that of receiving aircraft from the manufacturers, preparing them for issue, temporary storage and despatch to training and operational units. In April of that year, it was chosen as a final assembly point for the Airspeed Horsa Troop Carrying Glider. This was of all wood construction, ideal for component production by small local firms such as furniture manufacturers.

Aircraft were also dismantled for shipment abroad, but this work was carried out by No. 76 Maintenance Unit. It is said that up to thirty lorries a day left the airfield heading for the docks.

The year 1943 also saw the start of a large scale radio and radar modification programme which lasted almost to the end of the war.

May 1944 saw the maximum number of aircraft on the field - 573.

During the war years the Unit handled 7000 aircraft:-
2000 Barracudas, 500 Blenheims, 500 Hurricanes, 400 Horsas, 300
Spitfires and 250 Sea Otters and smaller numbers of miscellaneous
types, making 62 different types in all.

After the war it was used for storage of four engined aircraft and by autumn of 1945 there were 200 Lancasters filling the
airfield and dispersal areas.

During the next few years it was difficult to maintain the
full work force as men returned to local industry, but the Unit
remained very busy handling a large variety of aircraft which gradually changed with the development of jets.

In the 1960s there was a change to helicopters although there
were still many Canberras handled until the last one was flown away
in March 1972.

In 1971 it was announced that the Royal Navy would assume
responsibility for the airfield and the hand-over took place on 5th
April 1972.

In thirty-two years No. 15 Maintenance Unit handled 10,100
aircraft including nearly 500 helicopters and this covered 84
different types.

References and Sources of information

"The History of Number Fifteen Maintenance Unit"

Royal Air Force
Wroughton
1/4/1940 to 1/4/72

The British Forces helicopter maintenance centre at Wroughton
Its History and Present Role
Described by Alden P. Ferguson
(Aviation News)

THE RACING STABLES

by

Pamela McMeeking

)st certain that the establishment of Wroughton as
ing centre was due to the sporting activities of
erop Park. During the field sport season Mr Calley's
iates would gather together to partake in hunting,
g with greyhounds and horse racing on the downs.

purpose, in the early days, the sportsmen brought
)y wagon, later by canal and later still by rail and
n in the village. A number of cottages were built
commodate the sporting fraternity. From these
wners gradually left their horses here all the year
a groom to look after them and prepare them for the

:se humble beginnings Wroughton's connection with the
intil the village was renowned, throughout the
s a famous racehorse training centre with some flat
nly National Hunt. The horses were trained to stay
he downs lending themselves perfectly to schooling
to the fast finish.

and Stable

)na House had been the meeting place for the first
Church in the village, a Primitive Methodist Chapel and
was situated in the ancient way known as The Pitchens. The house
and stables are now demolished and replaced by a modern development.

In 1820 a horse from Barcelona defeated Mr Calley's horse
on the family's racecourse at Burderop - so obviously there was a
trainer or a groom here before Mr Leader.

William Leader - Trainer

William Leader was born in the village and was at Barcelona
from the early 1890's through to 1906, with twenty or so horses in
training for both the flat and steeplechasing. (see plate No 47.)

'Quilon', owned by Mr R. Lebaudy, won the 1894 Great Ebor
Handicap with Arthur Nightingall up and the Halliford Maiden
Hurdle Race. One of the most noted horses was 'Sweet Auburn', but
the most successful was 'Worcester', owned by Mr James Best who had
a small select breeding stud at Holt Castle just outside Bradford
on Avon. 'Worcester' carried off the Clarence and Doncaster Spring
Handicap and the Ascot Trial Stakes.

Some of the more successful owners with horses at Barcelona
were Mr T.G. Cartwright, Earl Cowley and Mr J.C. Joicey.

The Hon. Aubrey Craven Theophilus Robin Hood Hastings - Trainer

Aubrey Hastings was training at Woodmancote near Cheltenham
when he bought 'Asectic's Silver' for Prince Hatzfeldt. He trained
him and wasted severely to ride him to victory in the 1906 Grand
National. As a result of this success the delighted owner bought
Barcelona House and Stable for Aubrey Hastings.

He trained here with growing success and sent out three more National winners, the first 'Ally Sloper', the winner of seven chases including the Stanley and Valentine, won the Grand National in 1915 with Jack Anthony up, starting at 100-8. 'Ally Sloper' had the distinction of being owned by Lady Nelson, the first woman to own a National winner. 'Ally Sloper' was subsequently third in the 1917 National when it was won by another Wroughton horse. Jack and Ivor Anthony were the stable jockeys, living at Marston House in Devizes Road, now Mr K. Brown's the vetinary sugeon. (see plate No 41)

'Ballymacad' owned by Sir George Bullough, a member of the Jockey Club and the National Hunt Committee had his success in a substitute war National held at Gatwick in 1917 ridden by E. Driscoll, starting at 100-9. Sir George's racing colours were cerise with purple sleeves. (see plate No 42). Mrs Nolan, wife of the head travelling lad, made brow bands for the horses, to match the owners racing colours and often had to search Swindon to get the correct shade.

Lord Airlie in conjunction with Sidney Green owned 'Master Robert' who at one time was put to the plough and used in a dog cart but was sent to Aubrey Hastings and in the course of time improved so much as a jumper that he was entered for the National. Just before the big race 'Master Robert' bruised a bone in his hoof and Frank Cundell, the vetinary surgeon from Overtown House suggested that walking on the hard roads in Wroughton, without shoes would be the best treatment. Peter Roberts, the amateur jockey who lived at The Knole in Green's Lane, was to have been the jockey but 'opted out', and so it was left to Bob Trudgill to take 'Master Robert' to victory in 1924. Trudgill had extensive stitching in his leg and his exertions during the race split these open and he collapsed on dismounting. (see plate No 43).

Around this time the Hastings family moved to Woodham House, just a few yards from Barcelona. Here Aubrey Hastings, an international polo player, was able to keep his ponies with George Barber and Harry Trinder to look after them.

In 1922, Aubrey Hastings took on Ivor Anthony as Assistant Trainer. Ivor had been leading amateur jockey in 1904 and later as a professional was Champion Jockey in 1912, but was forced to retire after a bad fall. The stable, with about fifty horses in training, went from success to success and in 1927 'Brown Jack' joined them. (see plate No 44). 'Brown Jack' was bought for 750gns. for Sir Harold Wernher and came to Wroughton in July 1927. He took his place in the stables and Alfie Garratt became his lad.

Roger 'Tiny' Burford, a member of a local family living in the High Street, rode for the Hastings/Anthony stable for years and rode 'Brown Jack' in his first two victories over hurdles, in this country. Within nine months of arriving from Ireland, he achieved his owners wish, by winning the Cheltenham Champion Hurdle, ridden by Bilby Rees. At this meeting Hastings asked Steve Donoghue, the famous jockey, to watch 'Brown Jack', to see if he had any chance of winning on the flat. Donoghue agreed that he did and said that he would ride him. The famous partnership was formed and they were known as 'The Old Firm'. Around this time the number of horses in training was increased considerably, up to eighty or ninety, and every space had to be made available in order to stable them.

41   Ally Sloper ridden by Jack Anthony – Grand National 1915

42   Ballymacad ridden by E. Driscoll – Grand National 1917

43   Master Robert ridden by Bob Trudgill – Grand National 1924

44   Brown Jack ridden by Steve Donoghue – Queen Alexandra Stakes 1929-1934

'Brown Jack' was unplaced in his first race on the flat in May 1928, but before the year was out he had won the White Lodge Stakes, the Queen's Plate, the Ascot Stakes and the Hwfa Williams Memorial Stakes.

In May 1929 after playing polo at Cirencester Park, Aubrey Hastings was taken ill and died. This was a great loss to the village and the racing community. His stable was taken over by his widow and Ivor Anthony.

Ivor Anthony continued with 'Brown Jack's' training and in 1929 he won the Salisbury Cup, the Alexandra Stakes and the Nottingham Handicap.

'Brown Jack' was well used to the routine of the stable and the gallops at Burderop, so to keep him fresh it was arranged for him to be taken to neighbouring gallops. He visited Manton, Beckhampton, Ogbourne and Lambourn.

In 1930 'Mail Fist' was bought as a pace-maker for 'Brown Jack', and they became inseparable companions and were put in boxes side by side and always travelled together on their journeys to the racecourses. With the help of 'Mail Fist' 'Brown Jack' won the Alexandra Stakes, the Goodwood Cup and the Doncaster Cup.

'Brown Jack' and Steve Donoghue captured the hearts of the public and received gifts of apples, carrots and various cheeses plus many 'fan' letters, but 'Jack' was content to share Alfie's lunch of bread and cheese. He took to sitting on his manger whilst sleeping and Ivor and Alfie made a felt seat to make things more comfortable. 'Jack' didn't like this and spent most of the night removing it and in the morning it was found outside the stable, well chewed. 'Brown Jack' was turned out for the winter at his owners home, Thorpe Lubenham Hall, and when he returned to the stable to start the seasons training he still had a thick and straggley coat and looked nothing like the sleak racehorse the public had come to know. When visitors came to the stable to see the famous racehorse Ivor would pass him off as some old hack called 'Brown Jack' - much to everyone's amusement.

At the start of the 1931 season 'Brown Jack' was seven years old and still at his best. During this year he won the Chester Cup, the Queen Alexandra Stakes and the Ebor Handicap. In 1931 he won the Queen Alexandra Stakes and the Prince Edward Handicap and in 1933 the Rosebery Memorial Plate and the Queen Alexandra Stakes for the fifth time.

In 1934 'Brown Jack' was as fit and keen as ever, as he started his build up for the attempt to take the Queen Alexandra Stakes for the sixth time. His first race was at Lingfield Park followed by the Derbyshire Handicap - he was unplaced in both races and later third in the Chester Cup. Then came the big day! (see plate No 44)

On Friday the 22nd June 1934, all preparations made, the motor box was at the yard and 'Brown Jack' and 'Mail Fist' were led from their stables and with Ivor and Mrs Hastings and all the stable lads looking on, the two 'aged' horses were led into the box. Alfie joined them and Paddy Nolan, the head travelling lad, was at the wheel. There were shouts of good luck as the motor box pulled away.

'Brown Jack' was at Royal Ascot again. After the Royal Procession had driven past the stands and the preliminary races run and all was ready, Ivor saddled old 'Brown Jack' now 10 years old, but certainly there was no sign of age on that day. Alfie, proudly led him round the Parade Ring and Steve Donoghue was wearing the familiar colours of Sir Harold Wernher - green and yellow halved. Then came the time for Steve to mount 'Jack' and make their way to the start. Pat, Steve Donoghue's son, was riding 'Mail Fist' and wearing the same racing colours as his father.

Ivor Anthony could not watch 'Brown Jack' in his sixth attempt to win the race he had made his own, as the tension was too great. He heard the cry - their off! from his spot behind the stand, and sat there all alone until the cheers and cries told him that 'Brown Jack' and Steve Donoghue had done it! - they had won the Queen Alexandra Stakes for a record six times in succession, with the help of dear old 'Mail Fist'.

Ivor Anthony was in his place by the time the jubilant pair reached the winners enclosure. This was 'Brown Jack's' twenty-fifth win during his career and it would be his last as Sir Harold the owner of 'Brown Jack' and 'Mail Fist' had decided that this should be their last race. After all the congratulations, presentations and photographs the Wroughton Party made their way home after a most successful day.

Saturday the 28th July 1934 was the day 'Brown Jack' and 'Mail Fist' retired to their owners home. Alfie would miss his 'Jack', Ivor, who had trained him for most of his career, would miss that wise old boy, Mrs Hastings and the stable lads would certainly miss him too, and so of course would the villagers.

The Three Horse Shoes Inn was renamed the Brown Jack, as this was a favourite meeting place for the stable lads, and Mrs Hastings presented a picture of 'Brown Jack' to the Inn. The Barcelona Stable Lads soccer team was called the Brown Jacks and they were second in the Borough League. We now have the Brown Jack Stakes run at Royal Ascot over the same distance as the Queen Alexandra Stakes. On the fiftieth anniversary of the foaling of 'Brown Jack' Arkells, the Kingsdown Brewers, launched a new beer named the Brown Jack at the Three Tuns. Stuart Wilkins, was there and of course Alfie Garratt and once again the main topic of conversation was dear old 'Brown Jack'. In addition a cheese dish was named after him - 'Supreme de Chapon Brown Jack'.

Ivor Anthony trained for several Americans including Mr and Mrs Ambrose Clark.

'Kellsborough Jack' was to be entered for the National, but Mr Ambrose Clark was going through an unlucky period and so Ivor Anthony suggested that the horse should change hands. Mrs Ambrose Clark bought him for £1 and he won the 1933 National, ridden by Dudley Williams in record time in her colours of Light Blue, yellow chevrons, yellow sleeves and cap (see plate No 45).

Mr Hugh Lloyd-Thomas, a member of the British Embassy Staff, bought 'Royal Mail' and sent him to Ivor Anthony. He was successful in the 1937 Centenary Grand National with Evan Williams up. Evan had been the stable's secretary, but had turned into a first class jockey. 'Royal Mail' won many races including the Becher Chase. (see plate No 46).

45   Kellsborough Jack ridden by Danny Williams – Grand National 1933
with Ivor Anthony Trainer

46   Royal Mail ridden by Evan Williams – Centenary Grand National 1937
With Ivor Anthony Trainer and Stuart Wilkins

47   William Leader,Trainer.Schooling the horses up on the downs

48. Roger 'Tiny' Burford

49   Tom Leader Trainer at Fairwater House

Under the guidance of Ivor Anthony many races were won and I list below just a few of them:

1930	Boomlet	The Welsh Grand National
1931	Blue Vision	The Northumberland Plate
1933	Pebble Ridge	The Welsh Grand National
	Flaming	The Imperial Cup
	Blue Vision	The Chester Cup
	Chenango	The Emblem Chase
1935	Kellsborough Jack	The Scottish Grand National
1936	Sorley Boy	The Welsh Grand National
	Morse Code	The Grand Annual National Hunt
	Kellsborough Jack	The Champion Chase
1937	Morse Code	The National Hunt Chase
1938	Kellsborough Jack	The Cheltenham Champion Chase
	Morse Code	The Cheltenham Gold Cup
	Young Mischief	The Scottish Grand National
1940	Quartier Maitre	The Lincoln Handicap
1941	Poet Prince	The Cheltenham Gold Cup
1942	Red Rower	The Grand Annual Steeplechase
1945	Red Rower	The Cheltenham Gold Cup
1950	Klaxton	The Grand Military Gold Cup
1951	Klaxton	
1952	Klaxton	

Peter, Aubrey Hastings son, assisted Ivor Anthony from 1946. For several reasons the Stable was closed down in 1953. In preparation for the war an aerodrome had been built on part of the gallops, the volume of traffic had increased and two horses had to be put down because of injury. Ivor and Peter decided to train horses for the flat and moved to Kingsclere near Newbury.

The Manor and Stable

This beautiful old Elizabethan Manor House stood at the foot of Prior's Hill. It was let as flats in the early 1950's but after this was left unoccupied and allowed to fall into a sad state of disrepair. This fine old house had a preservation order on it, but it was allowed to be demolished to make way for a modern development. Thus we have lost the most outstanding house in the village.

Col. Robert Bradshaw Johnson - Trainer

Col. Johnson trained here from 1925 until he went to Australia in the early 1930's. He had a small stable with eight to ten horses with Frank Pearce as his Head Lad.

Major Frederick H Featherstonhaugh - Trainer

Major Featherstonhaugh was nicknamed 'Fred Feathers'. He trained here with about ten horses for a short time before becoming the Racing Manager to George V and moved to Windsor Great Park.

The Old Mill House and Stable

The Old Mill House still stands today, but where the waters once rushed to drive the massive mill stones, which now lie moss-covered in the garden, is a lovely oak-beamed Dining Hall.

Major Frederick Whitfield Barrett - Trainer

Shortly after the Great War Major Barrett came to Wroughton to set up his training stable at the Mill. The celebrated England Polo Player was nicknamed 'Rattle' as he was reputed to have broken every bone in his body. Major 'Rattle' Barrett, was with the 15th Kings' Hussars and later trained for George V. He often entertained the Prince of Wales, later the Duke of Windsor. Whilst in Wroughton the Prince was given riding lessons in the ways of steeplechasing by Ivor Anthony and went point to pointing with the Duke of Beaufort's Hunt.

Major Barrett sold the Mill House to the father of the present owner, Miss K.L. Crapp. Miss Crapp had a love for coaches and for a long time a Vale of White Horse Coach stood in the stable yard. Major Barrett moved to Wroughton Hall in Wharf Road, some may remember the 'green span' from the Mill House to the Hall, with just a couple of cottages in between.

'Silver Folly' bred and owned by Miss Crapp wore a rug once owned by Edward VII and 'Putting Green' carried the Kings colours and won flat races. In 1943 he won at Newmarket as a two year old for George VI. 'Putting Green' was later owned by Mr Harold Wilcox.

Wroughton Hall and Stable

Wroughton Hall was an old farm house which stood at the top of Wharf Road and was formerly known as Markham. Close by there was Markham Cottage and a short distance away Markham Road. The Hall was demolished and replaced by the Ellendune Shopping Centre.

Major Barrett continued to train for George V at the Hall. His horses included 'Lord Nugent' ridden by J. Sirett in the 1932 Rosebery Memorial Plate when he beat 'Brown Jack' and Steve Donoghue by three lengths.

Roger Burford rode out for Major Barrett together with Danny Morgan, who had a pretty bungalow built in Perry's Lane. Biddy, Major Barrett's daughter, was a familiar figure in the village exercising the racehorses. The Scouts have been a major interest in the Barrett family and the Scout meetings were held at the Hall until the late 1930's.

Another horse trained by Major Barrett was 'Marconi' which carried the colours of three Kings over the sticks; George V, Edward VIII and George VI.

Major Barrett was in command of the Home Guard from its formation in 1940 until he had to retire through age.

Fairwater House and Stable

Fairwater House and Stable still stands prominently in the High Street, but instead of the racehorses which were once seen in the Stable Yard there are Specialist Cars owned by Dick Lovett. (Plate 50).

Thomas Olliver - Trainer

Thomas Olliver was a great character and was born in Sussex. He was the finest steeplechase jockey of his time. He rode three horses to victory in the Grand National and coached a number of jockeys in the ways of steeplechasing. In the early 1860's Olliver moved to Wroughton to try his hand at training.

50   Fairwater House and Stable 1896

Tom's leading patron was Mr William Sheward Cartwright, who was Lord of the Manor of Llandaff in the County of Glamorgan. He named his horses after the hamlets in Llandaff and also after members of the Royal Family.

In 1863 'Fairwater' won the Northamptonshire Stakes with Harry Custance up and later the Ascot Gold Vase. 'Fairwater' gave his name to the House and Stable in the High Street. 'Ely' was one of the best horses that Mr Cartwright owned and he won the Prince of Wales' Stakes, the Doncaster Stakes, the Triennial, the Beaufort Cup and then dead heated for the 1865 Ascot Gold Cup with 'General Peel'. In the run off 'Ely' won by twelve lengths. It is this horse that lends its name to the Ely Inn in the High Street and is pictured in the sign outside. Incidentally, Tom Olliver was the Licensee there at one time. 'Ely' also won the Goodwood Cup and the Brighton Cup.

'Albert Victor' was placed in both the Derby and the Leger and won the Middle Park Stakes and many other valuable stakes. I list here some of the more successful of Mr Cartwright's horses. 'Louise Victoria', 'Victoria Alexandra', 'Maud Victoria','Albert Edward', 'George Albert', 'Fair Lyonese', and 'Caerou'.

Thomas Leader - Trainer

Tom Leader was born in the village and helped to manage Mr Cartwright's Stud, near Wroughton. He was sent to help old Tom Olliver but in fact took over the stable. Shortly afterwards Tom Olliver died and was buried in the Churchyard at Wroughton.

'George Frederick' was in training, but had not been getting enough exercise so young Tom Leader took him in hand and with Custance up he won the 1874 Derby, just as Olliver had predicted. The Wroughton Brass Band met the successful party at the Railway Station to escort 'George Frederick' and a stable companion back to their quarters in the High Street. Led by the trainer, Tom Leader, and his personal friends in conveyances with half of Wroughton following, the band played "See The Conquering Hero Comes".

Mr Cartwright presented the band with a pair of silver symbals suitably inscribed. The Licensing Trade in the village declared open house which meant that all had a free meal and drinks!!

Tom Leader also took on horses which he trained for National Hunt. The successful owners were Baron C de Tuyll, Capt. F Butler and a Mr Victors. Later there was also Col. Clitherow, Mr Fawcett and Messrs Joicey.

In 1880 Mr Cartwright died and in 1887 Tom Leader left the village to set up at Newmarket. There he renamed the stable, Wroughton House. At this stage his son Thomas Richard was 7 years old. We shall hear more of him later.

William Walters - Trainer

William Walters also trained at Fairwater and for some of the time whilst Tom Leader was there. It seems likely that they trained together between 1880 and 1887. When Walters left Wroughton, he too went to Newmarket, to Primrose Cottage.

Edward A Craddock - Trainer

Edward A Craddock trained at Fairwater after Leader and Walters left for Newmarket and stayed through to the early months of 1900, with a fairly small string of horses.

Craddock trained 'Father Flynn', with much success, but unfortunately his owner sold him just before he won the 1892 Grand National. 'Van der Berg' was placed twice in the National, a second and a third. 'Aesop' won the 1894 Grand Military Gold Cup. 'Exodus' won the National Hunt Steeplechase four times and 'Earl Ronan' won nearly all the open banking races in the West Country in one season. Other horses trained by Craddock were 'Fiana' 'The Fawn' and 'Night of the Galtese'.

Thomas Richard Leader - Trainer

Thomas Richard Leader already mentioned, trained here from 1900 until he went to the War. Whilst he was away his wife, a daughter of a Swindon butcher named Keylock, took the family to Newmarket to live. When Thomas returned from the war he trained at Newmarket and the family has lived there ever since. Roger 'Tiny' Burford was at this stable until Thomas Richard moved to Newmarket, and then he joined the Barcelona Stable.

The Paddocks

The Paddocks in Devizes Road backed on to the Barcelona Stable. It had a thatched roof, but is now tiled. There were thatched loose boxes and stables all around the yard and they extended into the paddock at the rear of the cottage.

Mr William Courtenay Clack - Trainer

Mr Clack of Devon set up in the village with a small stable in the 1890's. Three of his horses that were successfully trained for the flat were 'Marin', 'Porte Bonheur' and 'Portrush'; he was more successful with his hurdlers. 'Deela' and 'Horatio' were victorious at Torquay in 1895. 'Skelton' was a frequent winner and also 'Cardinal'.

'Skelton' won the Heythorp Selling Steeplechase at the Banbury Hunt Meeting and this was followed by a similar win at the South Berks gathering. 'Skelton' won at Cardiff in the April and again in the October followed by the County Selling Steeplechase. 'Marin' won the Maiden Plate at Birmingham. 'Deela' won twice at Torquay in April 1895 in the Ladies Handicap Hurdle and the St Marychurch Hurdle Plate.

Arthur Gordon - Trainer

Arthur Gordon was nicknamed 'Moppy' because of his large head of hair and was quite a character, wearing bright clothes, loud checks and plus fours. 'Moppy' trained here for five or six years after a short period with his brother, Robert, at Warleigh.

Montague Bernard Savill - Trainer

Monty Savill trained here from the early 1920's through to 1948, he had a stable of about twenty horses. Before taking up training he drove racing cars at Goodwood and always drove a Bentley Motor Car whilst at Wroughton.

'Cold Comfort' is the only horse I have found that Monty Savill trained, there must have been more, but none has come to light as yet.

Warleigh House and Stable

Warleigh House is a large Victorian house standing in its own grounds, reached by a private road from The Pitchens. Until recently there were a number of stable buildings, but now only one wooden block stands.

Robert Gordon - Trainer

Robert Gordon trained here from 1901 until 1938, his brother was with him for a few years before he moved to The Paddocks. Robert had twenty or so horses in training.

51   The Barcelona Stable Lads with Aubrey Hastings,Trainer

52   The Barcelona Stable Lads with Ivor Anthony,Trainer & Mrs Hastings

Robert's head lad was Ginger Mariner, who used to delight the customers at the Brown Jack Inn with his Irish Blarney.

Robert Ernest Davey was apprenticed to Robert Gordon and was third on his first mount 'Irish Oak' at Cheltenham in 1907.

Jean Stratford - Trainer

In recent years Jean trained 'Spiritus Royal' at Warleigh, making use of the one remaining stable block and the paddock.

Later Jean trained 'Star Cloud' a chaser and 'Capitalist' a hurdler. Jean and Nicki Durnford would ride the horses out, for their daily exercise up on the downs.

Millbrook House and Stable

Millbrook House stands in Devizes Road and is perhaps one of the oldest cottages in the village. Around the turn of the century there were a great number of thatched loose boxes and stables which were used in the first world war as a Remount Depot. The sick and wounded horses were brought here to recover and were then returned to the war.

Until recently there were still a number of tiled stables, but some of these have now been demolished, leaving one for the owners own horses and two at the back of the house which Mrs J Patterson uses for her Riding School.

Mr William Hatt - Trainer

Bill Hatt trained at Millbrook House, but I have no other information regarding this trainer.

Overtown Stud

Mr Francis Lawrence Cundell, a vetinary surgeon, came to Overtown in the early 1920's and set up a stud.

One horse that stood at Overtown in the 1930's was 'Noble Star' by 'Hapsburg' out of 'Hesper' by 'Herodote'. Frank and Len Cundell bought 'Noble Star' and Len trained him. In 1931 he won the Ascot Stakes, Goodwood Stakes, Cesarewitch and the Jockey Club Cup. He then retired and stood at Overtown.

Shortly after the second world war, Sir Henry Calley, came to Overtown.

Sir Henry, provides a service to people who wish to breed racehorses, but don't have their own stables. He boards mares in between visits to the stallions and their offspring.

Among the winners bred at the Stud are the Hon. A Samuel's 'Filles de Retz' who won the 2000 guineas in 1956. 'Raffingora' (whose dam 'Cameo' bred no fewer than eight winners) who broke the record for five furlongs at Epsom and still holds it, who was the sire of 'Overtown' who won twice at Newmarket and the Norfolk Stakes at Royal Ascot as a two year old. Sir Henry gave him the name 'Overtown' because his dam 'Tender Courtesan' and his grandam 'Court Caprice', were all bred here and his great grandam 'Whimbrel', the property of the late General Sir Miles Dempsey, was a great favourite of Sir Henry's and was at the Stud for many years. She bred several winners including 'Whimsical' the dam of 'Bombazine' who was dam of 'Brunei', who won the St Leger. Another good mare was Mr J.R. Henderson's 'Acclis' who bred several winners including 'Acquire' who is the dam of that good sprinter 'Shellaston Park'.

To keep the flag flying in a rather more modest way is 'Still Hope'
a son of 'Shilly Shally' and grandaughter of 'Whimbrel' who won races
on the flat, over hurdles and fences before he was six years old.

Overtown Manor

Rosemary White is the only person in the village who trains
today and she has ridden several of her horses to victory.

I have found the names of eight trainers, but do not know
where their stables were - can you help?

1851	John Jannton
1851 - 1871	John Stinton
1859	Henry Curlewis
1861	Henry L. Ellison
1861	Edward Enock
1861	Edmund Jones
1875	George Eatwell
1920	William Hartell

There were nearly one hundred stable lads employed in the various
stables who all lived in the village. Wroughton had its own racing
saddler, William Wykes. There were several shoeing smiths or farriers,
Bill Blackford was at Barcelona Stable and was pictured with his son
(see plate No 50).

John Searle, a reporter for several of the sporting papers,
would go to the Post Office at 8.00 a.m. to report which horses had been
out for exercise and how they were going.

Since the stables left Wroughton some of the larger houses have
been demolished - whilst they were here these buildings were provided
for - if they had stayed perhaps they would have preserved the village
itself.

The Racing Stables played a major part in the history of
Wroughton, bringing in money, employing a great number of people,
providing work for specialist trades and pleasure to many many more people.
When Barcelona Stable closed down and the last racehorse and trainer
left, the heart went out of the village.

References and Sources of Information

Wroughton Monthly
A Guide to Your Village 4th Edition 1973.
Racing Illustrated 1896
Brown Jack written by R.C. Lyle 1934
A Swindon Retrospect by Frederick Large 1970
The Cheltenham Gold Cup by John Welcome 1957
Riding Recollections and Turf Stores by Henry Custance 1894
Biographical Encyclopaedia of British Flat Racing by Roger Mortimer,
Richard Onslow and Peter Willett
The Encyclopaedia of Steeplechasing by Roger Mortimer
W.W. Rouch & Co for their kind permission to use their photographs for
plates 41, 42, 43, 44 & 45.

53. The High Street looking West

54. The High Street looking East. Women are collecting water at the
stand pipe near the sign post.

55. Manor Farm, also known as Ducks Farm or Smiths Farm. Demolished in the last few years.

56. Coventry Farm. This was near the site of the Iron Horse until the 1960's

57. The South side of High Street before the fire of 1896

58. Looking towards Fairwater House, showing racehorses.

59. Church Hill showing the Post Office at the turn of the century

60. Church Hill viewed from the downs. This area is known as 'the Castle'

61. Priors Hill corner, showing the Forge cottage and the Inn then called the 3 Horse Shoes

62. Swan Inn corner Priors Hill. A hundred years ago there were many tiny cottages on the present car park

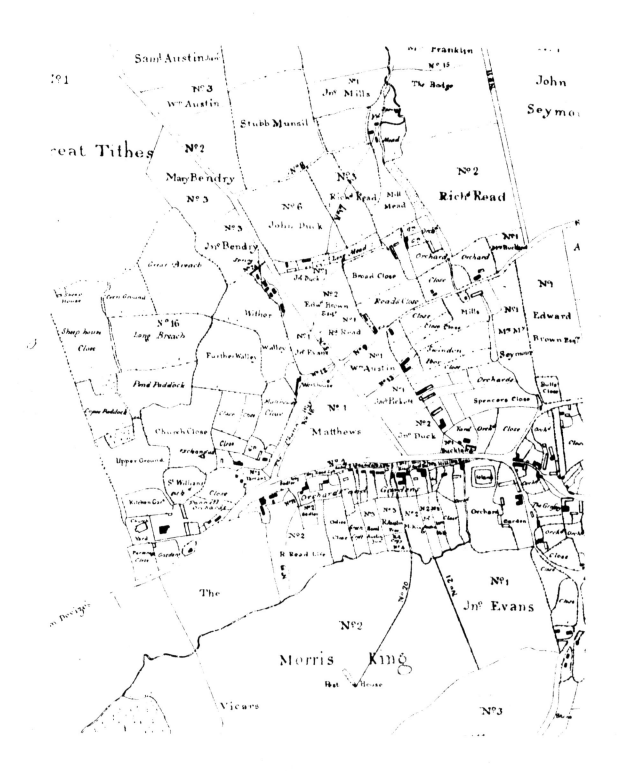

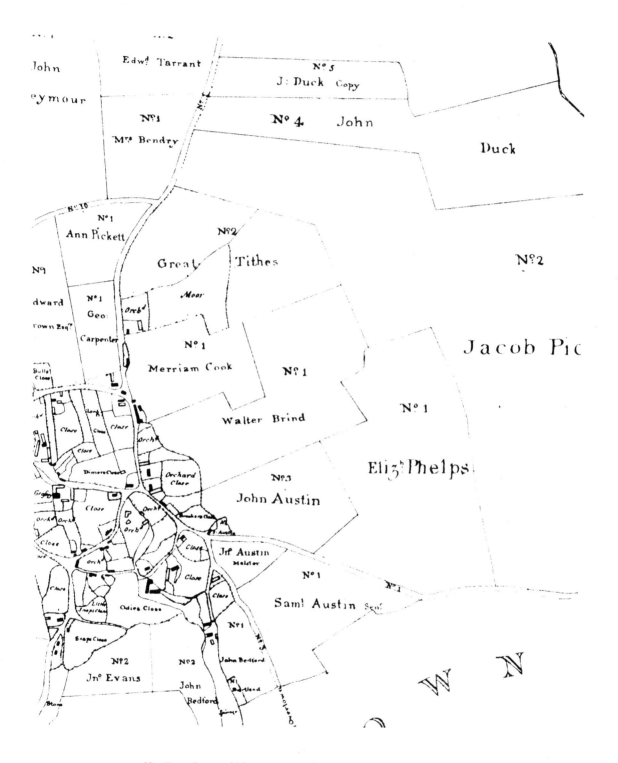

65. Wroughton village centre in 1795. An enlargement of Plate 34.

63. Wharf Road around 1900. Only a low wall with railings still survives, and the 'Towers' where the boy is sitting

64. The Manor House, Priors Hill. Demolished by 1960